Table of Contents

KV-373-967

Paris Travel Guide!

The Ultimate Tourist's Guide to Sightseeing, Adventure & Partying in Paris

Copyright

Introduction

I want to thank you and congratulate you for downloading the book, "*Paris Travel Guide! The Ultimate Tourist's Guide to Sightseeing, Adventure & Partying in Paris.*"

This book contains a comprehensive guide to all the wonders that Paris has to offer. It aims to ensure you get the most out of your visit, leaving absolutely nothing undiscovered. From must-see tourist attractions to unique nightlife experiences, this book has you covered!

The bustling streets of Paris will lead you to one stunning vista after another, from the sunset at the highest point of the Eiffel Tower to the quaint cafés that sprout up at intervals along the sidewalk. Known as the City of Light, Paris has the uncanny ability to appeal to each and every soul both young and old, attracting millions of tourists from all four corners of the world.

Here is a place where fashionistas, art enthusiasts, history buffs, chronic partiers, and thrill-seekers unite under the same azure sky, sharing the fragrant Parisian air. Prepare to go on an amazing journey through the busy capital and to lose yourself in history. But don't forget to leave some room in your itinerary for the underground Parisian nightlife. With so many otherworldly sights and sounds to explore, the fun in Paris never ends!

Within the pages of this book are the places and activities waiting for you in the endlessly beating heart of France. Go to where the lights shine bright, to the out-of-the-way holes in the wall, to within inches of da Vinci's priceless masterpieces, and the mammoth edifices deep in the core of Paris. Drop a few euros in the fashion district, get off the beaten path to the hills, check out Paris Fashion Week, or visit the bakeries selling delightful pastries. Leave nothing omitted! I hope you enjoy this travel guide, but chances are, you'll enjoy your stay in Paris much more!

Thank you again for downloading this book. I hope you enjoy it!

Chapter 1: Paris in a Nutshell

An illuminated emerald of Europe, Paris sits on the Seine River in the northern environs of France. Home to over two million Parisians scattered over 40 square miles of terrain, both concrete jungle and natural earth, Paris is a small yet awe-inspiring place.

Paris earned the nickname "The City of Light" for itself, being the first European city to adopt gas-powered street lightning, and due to its role in the Age of Enlightenment—an era characterized by an emphasis in reason, analysis, and individualism. By as early as the 1860s, Paris was lit by tens of thousands of gas lamps—a feat deemed nearly impossible during that time.

Paris is internationally known as a fashion capital and a hub of architecture. Its three-star restaurants, haute cuisine, and architectural landmarks are just a few of the capital's most noteworthy points of interest. Paris is also home to the most visited museum in the entire world, the Musée du Louvre, a shining symbol of the great city. Other notable landmarks include the Eiffel Tower and Notre Dame Cathedral, both continuing to play a chief role in Parisian tourism.

France is ranked at the very top of the chart of most visited countries, with United States coming in at a close second. In 2014 alone, France welcomed approximately 83.7 million international tourists, with the majority travelling to Paris. In terms of most popular cities to visit, Paris comes in third behind London and Bangkok.

Origins

In the middle of the 3rd century BC, a Celtic sub-tribe by the name of Parisii arrived in Paris via the River Seine. The river became a trade area between Paris and other nearby river towns. The Parisii minted their own gold coins for that particular purpose.

In 52 BC, the Romans conquered old Paris, bringing prosperity. The small Roman town was renamed Lutetia. Theaters, temples, and an amphitheater were built along the Paris basin. From the end of the Roman empire arose a new town name, Parisius. Saint Denis introduced Christianity to the growing city where he became the very first Bishop of Paris.

Fun Fact: Île de la Cité is the official birthplace of Paris. If you find yourself in the area during your visit, try to imagine how the island must have looked in 53 BC.

Paris Today

Over the centuries, Paris has grown into a thriving capital replete with its own unique culture and cityscape that sets it apart from other notable French cities. From the aftermath of wars, the city rose from the ashes like a phoenix, gradually restoring and building itself into the European gem it is today. Now Paris is a place where old meets new.

Past conflicts gave the city its resilience; as a beautiful result, incredible monuments and charming architecture now honeycomb the City of Light. To stand in Paris is to stand in both new-fashioned and ancient times, a place where modern marvels and amazing historical feats collide to form a one-of-a-kind city that rivals all other capitals in cultural scope and charm. Heavenly food, the Seine, the iconic landmarks, and chic shopping are all the reasons you need to vacation in Paris.

If you're planning a visit to Paris, having a thorough knowledge of its multicolored history is definitely useful. But since Paris is a whole new world, the city may bring about a hefty dose of culture shock to Western tourists. To soften the blow—one that's both pleasant and shocking in equal measure—it's helpful to know the ins and outs and full particulars of the great capital. Here is Paris in a nutshell.

Fun Fact: In the past, Japanese tourists in Paris have been sent back to Japan as a result of the Paris Syndrome—an extreme form of culture shock. Unlike you, they probably didn't read a comprehensive guide to Paris beforehand.

Climate

The climate in Paris is of a temperate nature completely free of harsh weather, which some say further adds to the city's natural charm. Spring in Paris brings a garden-like feel to the city as the air becomes infused with a medley of floral aromas, making it ideal for the hopeless romantic.

Leaving acres of greenery and blossoms in its wake, Spring lends Paris mild temperatures which allow for a light sweater and leisurely stroll. Spring showers tend to come and go every three days, but there is never a torrential downpour during the season. When it rains over Paris, it is said to have a beautiful effect on the hundreds of twinkling lights scattered about.

Summer makes Paris a tourist hotspot, particularly in June when daytime temperatures are warm and tolerable enough for outdoor adventure. June also brings about the longest days of the Parisian year, with the sun typically setting no earlier than 10 p.m. During the summer months of July and August, Paris teems with tourists. Street side cafés become a favorite haunt for both locals and international visitors.

Summer is a high travel season with skyrocketing airfare and hotel accommodations, but the French Open and Tour de France promises an unrivaled summer experience in Paris. Bastille Day on July 14th is accompanied by a huge celebration and a fireworks display behind the Eiffel Tower—an experience like no other. Be sure to pack lightly to leave enough room for the summer sales!

Authentic Paris can be experienced in autumn when there are fewer tourists and less congestion on the boulevards. Fall enables travelers to witness the ordinary goings-on in the city as Parisians resume work and grade school students return to school after summer vacation. Paris is windiest during the fall season, with cool, crisp weather that's conducive to romantic walking. As the season makes its transition to winter, cool weather gives way to frost and the occasional snow. Sunshine becomes scarce, though temperatures remain just above freezing. Festive lights are strung up throughout the capital, adding yet another layer of charm and illumination to the Parisian backdrop. Winter is the cheapest time to visit Paris, but don't forget your peacoat!

Geography

The city of Paris is divided into 20 distinct areas called "arrondissements." The arrondissements of Paris are laid out in a spiral pattern, with the first nestled right smack dab in the middle of the city. Parisians usually refer to the different areas of their city according to the arrondissement. The Seine River flows through the center of Paris, dividing the city into Left Bank and Right Bank. Traditionally, the Left Bank is the artistic, chaotic side while the Right Bank tends to be more business-like and orderly.

Administration

Being a capital, Paris is the seat of France's national government. There are two chief officers in France, the president and prime minister. The President of France's official residence is at the Élysée Palace while the Hôtel Matignon serves as the office of the Prime Minister. Both houses of the French Parliament, the Senate and the Assemblée Nationale, are situated on the Left Bank.

City Government

Once upon a time, Paris was governed by representatives of the king, emperor, or president of France. Now, mayors are elected to govern the city; Paris' current mayor is Anne Hidalgo.

Paris voters don't elect the mayor of the city. Instead, the voters of each of the 20 arrondissements elect the Council of Paris, which is composed of 163 members. These council members then select the mayor. Each arrondissement has its own town hall, with the number of members in one arrondissement dependent on the population.

Fun Fact: There stands a replica of the Statue of Liberty in Paris that faces the Statue of Liberty in the United States, a symbol of friendship between the two nations.

Police Force

The Prefecture of Police in Paris is primarily responsible for Paris security. The organization supervises the officers of the Police Nationale in Paris who patrol the city as well as three neighboring departments. Complete with emergency service providers, a fire brigade, and riot control, the Prefecture of Police in Paris is headquartered on Place Louis Lépine.

Currently, there are 30,000 Parisian officers under the prefecture, boasting a fleet of over 6,000 police vehicles. A visit to Paris enables you to see the officers in action throughout the streets, on horseback, motorcycles, boats, and cars. One unique aspect of Parisian police is their upheld duty of verifying that at least *one* bakery is open in every neighborhood during the summer months. Crime in Paris is no different than that of large cities. Fortunately, violent crime and political violence are rare.

Cityscape

What sets Paris apart in terms of architecture is the standing monuments left behind by past rulers which have never been destroyed—neither by war nor catastrophe. The avenues of the city are characterized by a neutral color palette, the use of Lutetian limestone, aligned street fronts, and tree-lined boulevards. The apex of the world-renown Eiffel Tower offers 360° views of the entire city.

Fun Fact: There is only one stop sign in Paris, and it's located in the 16th arrondissement. The Parisian traffic system is based on a "right of way" scheme.

Housing

Housing in Paris is not for the miser, but ideal for the spendthrift. To put things into perspective, Paris is the eighth most expensive city to live in. Luxury housing, though offering all creature comforts, is typically reserved for the nouveau riche. The most expensive and sought-after streets in Paris is the quai des Orfèvres situated in the 6th arrondissement. To make a home for yourself on this street, be ready to shell out $2115 per square feet. The majority of Parisians is a rent-paying population, with most of them residing in studio and space-conscious two-bedroom apartments.

Fun Fact: There's a Frenchman living in the 14th arrondissement who invites complete strangers—including tourists—to dinner at his house on a weekly basis. Weird, but admittedly, it would turn a notch up on your Parisian adventure meter. If you're interested in an invitation, all you have to do is register on website at http://www.jim-haynes.com/contact/. He's been having dinner parties with strangers for thirty years.

The Parisian Economy

Paris is described as one of the engines of the global economy. The city's GDP in 2014 was calculated at over €600 billion (approximately $660 billion), making Paris the fourth largest in the world. One survey rated Paris as one of the most expensive cities in which to purchase goods and services.

Paris also has one of the highest income per capita in the world. Paris alone accounts for approximately 30% of France's wealth. The Parisian economy is mainly a service economy. Paris ranks second behind Tokyo with the highest number of Global 500 companies.

Fun Fact: France was the first country to produce license plates, which were developed in Paris.

Employment

Employment rates in Paris goes as follows:

- 59% of the Parisian workforce is in transportation, commerce, and marketing.
- 27% in human health, social work, education, and public administration
- 9% in manufacturing
- 6% in construction
- 0.5% in agriculture

Considered a wealthy city, the average net household income in Paris today is €36,085, or $40,000. Coincidentally, Paris also houses some of the poorest neighborhoods in France, mostly on the eastern bank. In these destitute areas, households earn no more than €977 per month, approximately $1000, which is the official poverty line in the nation.

Tourism

In 2014 alone, Paris welcomed nearly 23 million tourists. This number is clear proof of the capital's popularity as an international tourist destination. Most tourists visit from the United States, followed by the United Kingdom and Asia. During 2014, tourists spent a whopping €13.60 billion in Paris, which is equivalent to 14.4 billion U.S. dollars.

Fun Fact: As of today, there are 6,100 streets

crisscrossing Paris. Are you prepared to walk them all? The shortest Parisian street, *Rue de Degrés*, is only 18.9 feet long!

Tourist Hotspots

Parisian monuments and museums attract the most tourist activity annually. The five most popular tourist attractions in Paris per year from greatest to least are as follows:

1. Notre Dame Cathedral: 14 million visitors
2. Basilique du Sacré-Cœur: 10.5 million visitors
3. The Louvre Museum: 9.2 million visitors
4. Eiffel Tower: 6.7 million visitors
5. Musée d'Orsay: 3.5 million visitors

Overall, the city of Paris contains the most visited monuments in France.

Fun Fact: There's a coffee shop in Paris that jacks up the price of your coffee if you forget to say "Please" and "Thank you." We don't know which one it is, so just to be safe, don't forget your manners whenever you visit a Parisian café.

Hotels

Among the 1,570 hotels in Paris, 55 are rated five-star. These five-star resorts are located primarily near the Champs-Élysées. One of the most famous luxury hotels in Paris is the Hotel Meurice, the city's premier grand hotel which opened its doors in 1817. Other notable Parisian hotels include the Hôtel Ritz, Hôtel Crillon, and the

Hotel Bristol—all defined by luxury in its purest form. If you happen to have several thousand euros lying around, you might be able to afford a night's stay in one of these prestigious Parisian hotels. Lucky for you, even the three-star Parisian hotels offer enough luxury for your champagne taste on a blue-jean budget.

Parisian Culture

Though widely known as the City of Light, Paris has also acquired a reputation as the City of Art. For hundreds of years, artists from far and wide have flocked to Paris in search of artistic education and inspiration from its vast array of galleries. Italian Renaissance artists made a profound impact on the development of Parisian art forms during the 16th century. During the Baroque period of dramatic grandeur, French royals adorned their palaces with reliefs and sculptures built by skilled Parisian artists.

Some of the finest artists to come out of Paris include Pierre Mignard, Claude Monet, Nicolas Coustou, and Girardon. Pablo Picasso of Spain and Vincent van Gogh of the Netherlands are two of the greatest artists who ever lived; surprisingly, they owe their fame to Paris.

Fun Fact: Up until 2012, it was illegal for Parisian women to wear trousers. Speaking of illegal, child beauty pageants are banned throughout the entire country of France.

Museums

Museums play a significant role in Parisian culture. Paris is home to over 150 museums both world-renown and unsung. Parisian museums house some of the world's most famous artifacts and works of art. A visit to Paris wouldn't be complete without standing before the Mona Lisa in the Louvre, going for a hair-raising underground stroll through the Catacombs of Paris, and standing in the same room with long-extinct dinosaurs—albeit in fossil form.

Fun Fact: "Fun" isn't actually the right word for this fact, but I'll let you be the judge. In the late 1700s, a French doorman got lost in the underground maze of the Catacombs of Paris. According to tradition, he had been in search for liquor. His body was found 11 years later.

Theater

Theater occupies a special place in Parisian culture. Many A-list actors of today found fame in French television. Bobino, a major theater in Paris which doubles as a concert hall, honed some of France's greatest musical legends. If you're a fan of opera and ballet, I recommend adding at least one opera house to your itinerary. Opéra Garnier and the newer Opéra Bastille are the largest and most popular in Paris. The latter is, in fact, considered to be the most celebrated opera house in the world.

Fun Fact: The French government prohibited

Tom Cruise from becoming an honorary citizen due to the actor's affiliation with Scientology.

Literature

Epistolae by Gasparinus de Bergamo, was the first ever book printed in France. Translated to *Letters*, it was actually published in Paris in 1470. Since the dawn of French literature, Paris has served as the hub of the French publishing industry. Some of the most illustrious poets and writers of all time came straight out of Paris, including Gustave Flaubert, Alexandre Dumas, Jules Verne, Victor Hugo, and Voltaire—all of which, you may agree, are common household names.

Fun Fact: Victor Hugo's famous work, *Les Misérables*, was written while he was in exile during the Second Empire. Another of his works, *The Hunchback of Notre Dame*, sparked the renovation of the Notre Dame de Paris.

Music

Paris has a rich musical history which was influenced by notable composers like Jean-Baptiste Lully and, even more familiar, Debussy. Ballet music made headlines out of Paris during the 1800s. Bal-musette is a form of French music and dance that gained popularity in the late 1800s. Today, it remains the most popular style of dance in France. You will see modernized forms of bal-musette dance in the jazz corners of Paris complete with accordion bands.

Fun Fact: French radio stations are required to play 40% of French music during prime hours.

Nightlife

The Parisian nightlife began as early as the 19th century in the form of cabaret dance. The cabaret trend began with the opening of La Chat Moir in the Montmartre district of Paris. Nightlife grew in scope upon the opening of the Moulin Rouge, which featured operettas in which Parisian women performed a type of cabaret dance involving an indecent display of skin. The Parisian nightlife evolved into jukebox bars, then discos, and eventually into the typical raves and pop-music clubs of Paris today.

For Parisians, a night at a club is the normal thing to do after a long work week. For tourists, however, Paris offers a one-of-a-kind club experience for the daring side within everyone. Bar-hopping is an absolute must-do in Paris while you're there, but only if you're wild and willing. If not, don't fret! The Marais district is a favorite haunt among those who prefer a watered-down form of clubbing. Paris offers a diverse array of bars that conform to both extroverts and introverts. Whether your aim is to wind down and relax, or get turned up and flirt, there's a nightclub in Paris tailored to your tastes.

Fun Fact: There are 1,124 bars in Paris. You may not have time for a drink at each bar during your stay, but just remember to visit one of the 1,784 Parisian bakeries at your disposal for a quick sober-me-up. Even more convenient, there are 181 places in the city where you can get an espresso for a measly €1 to shake off your hangover. That's four quarters and a dime!

Parisian Cuisine

Beginning in the late 18th century, Paris became known around the world for its haute cuisine, a style that is the cooking equivalent of haute couture. Countless restaurants throughout Paris continue to make a name for themselves due to their unique method of skillfully preparing food and presenting them in an impressive artful manner. If your travel funds allow for authentic haute cuisine at an award-winning French restaurant, consider dining at Ledoyen amidst the gardens of the Champs-Élysées or the Tour d'Argent on the Quai de la Tournelle.

Of course, there are also many budget-friendly fine-dining experiences to choose from. Among these relatively inexpensive Parisian restaurants are Le Dôme Café, Les Deux Magots, and Café de la Rotonde, which are all located on the Left Bank. They're all wonderful options from the 20th century for the budget-conscious tourist.

Fun Fact: Bistro restaurants originated in Paris. They're characterized by moderately priced meals in a simple, modest setting. If you're a fan of home-style cooking and bound to a budget, bistros are the perfect choice.

Fashion

Since the 19th century, Paris has been an international high-fashion capital. Haute couture, a dressmaking style of designing high-quality fashion, has deep roots in Paris. I'm willing to bet that you have a prized Chanel bag or Dior sunglasses—or perfume, at the very least. These fashion houses are one of the two largest in the world, and they're headquartered in Paris.

Paris Fashion Week, a clothing trade show that is well-known even among the not-so-fashion-conscious, is held twice a year in January and July. Louis Vuitton, Cartier, and Hermès are all Parisian developers of luxury fashion accessories. Maybe you could knock on the CEO of Hermès' door during your visit and humbly ask him to put a cheaper price tag on that Birkin day bag you've been eyeing.

Fun Fact: Paris is home to L'Oréal, the largest cosmetics company in the world. Hey, you might even have traces of Paris on your face through L'Oréal foundation!

Festivals and Holidays

If you time your vacation right, you just might experience some of the greatest festivals in Europe. Every year on July 14th, a military parade takes place on the Champs-Élysées followed by a spectacular fireworks display in celebration of Bastille Day. Or perhaps you could party in the Seine with locals during the pleasantly blistering Parisian summer when the river is converted into a beach complete with sand, deck chairs and palm trees! This annual festival, called Paris-Plages, starts in mid-July, and continues throughout the summer up until mid-August.

Fun Fact: In an effort to promote safe sex during rowdy festivals as well as in school, the Town Hall provided the city with condom vending machines. There are a total of 31 of these machines scattered throughout Paris—in universities, public toilets, and even in metros. Ninety-six percent of French high schools have these vending machines in their halls—as though they were gumball machines.

Religion

As the seat of the Archbishop of Paris, the Notre Dame Cathedral is a symbol of Catholicism in France. The majority of the Parisian population has identified with the Roman Catholic faith since the early Middle Ages. Two official pilgrimage sites exist in Paris, one being the Basilica of Sacré-Cœur, and the other being the Chapel of Our Lady of the Miraculous Medal. There are 110 Catholic schools located in Paris, boasting a total of 75,000 students.

Though Catholicism is the predominant faith among Parisians, there are also Jewish, Muslim, and Buddhist communities throughout the city, including one Hindu temple in the 18th arrondissement.

Sports

Stade Français and Paris Saint-Germain F.C. are the most popular sport clubs in Paris. The largest stadium in France, Stade de France, hosts football, rugby union, and track and field events. Another popular French sport is tennis; the French Open is a major tennis tournament held in Paris over two weeks during the early summer months. Two sporting events to look forward to in Paris are the UEFA Euro 2016 and the 2017 IIHF World Championship.

Fun Fact: The most popular bicycle race in the world, the Tour de France, always finishes in Paris on the Champs-Élysées.

Infrastructure

Paris' extensive road network is comprised of over 1,200 miles of motorways and highways. Three orbital freeways circle the city: the Périphérique, the A86 motorway, and the Francilienne motorway. By train, London is only two hours away. Parisian roads lead to Brussels in just three hours; Frankfurt in six; and Barcelona in twelve. Approximately 270 miles of cycle paths are reserved for bicyclists.

Fun Fact: A bicycle sharing system called Vélib' is available for use for both locals and tourists. The system has 1,800 bicycle parking systems distributing over 20,000 public bicycles for rent.

Air and Sea Transportation

Fourteen airports serve the city of Paris, with four of those being international airports. The Paris-Charles de Gaulle is Paris' major and most busiest airport; it's also the center for Air France, the country's primary flag carrier.

In all of France, Paris is the most active transport area due to the five rivers connected to the Seine River by canal. The cargo is handled by the Autonomous Port of Paris.

Rail Transportation

Opened in 1900 and comprising 300 stations connected by 133 miles of rails, the Métro is Paris' official subway system. The Métro carries 9 million passengers on a daily basis, making it the most widely used transport system in France. In fact, the Métro is the sixth most used transport system in the world, transporting over 1.5 billion Parisians and tourists every year. In one day, the Métro travels a mind-boggling 600,000 miles. That's approximately *six* times around the earth! To put that into perspective, the moon is only 238,855 miles away from where you're standing now.

Fun Fact: Each metro stop in Paris has a theme which primarily involves key historical figures associated with the city. With the help of Google and a little attention to detail, you'll learn a great deal of Parisian history just by riding the Métro. What makes this possible is the fact that you only need one metro ticket which you can use for every single metro line.

So if you're feeling up to it, leave a spot open in your itinerary to travel Paris underground for a full day.

Parks and Gardens

Modern day Paris is home to 421 municipal parks and gardens, spanning a total area of over 7400 acres. The most popular gardens are the Tuileries Garden and Luxembourg Garden, created in 1564 and 1612, respectively. A newer park that is quickly becoming a tourist hotspot is the Promenade des Berges de la Seine. What set it apart from other beautiful Parisian parks are the floating gardens that offer an incredible panoramic view of Paris' landmarks.

Fun Fact: There are 470,000 trees in the whole of Paris, and they're all referenced and measured. Half of the trees in Paris are in the city's parks and gardens.

Chapter 2: A Well-Spent Day at the Louvre

The Louvre is nestled between the bustling communities of trendy Les Halles and chic Faubourg Saint-Honoré. The latter, though relatively narrow and nondescript, is the high-end fashion district of Paris. It's often cited as being one of the poshest streets in the world. Once belonging to French royalty, Rue Faubourg Saint-Honoré now acts as innkeeper to every major fashion house in the world.

Source:
http://impressivemagazine.com/2013/06/20/interesting-facts-about-the-louvre-museum/

Alongside high-fashion, the street is also home to the Élysée Palace, the official residence of the French president. As though that weren't enough, Rue Faubourg Saint-Honoré also has foreign ambassadors calling it home. The classy street is just as beloved to modern day fashionistas as it was to the royal mistresses of bygone times. Faubourg Saint-Honoré is easily one of the only places in Paris where both fashionistas and important political figures share pavements.

In contrast, Les Halles has a more laidback atmosphere and is home to the hottest neighborhoods in Paris. Once a market district with a really bad vermin infestation, Les Halles is now home to mellow cafés, hip bars, and trendy shops, making it a favorite haunt among Parisian hipsters.

Things to do at the Louvre

The Louvre is easily the most visited area in Paris, and for good reason! Below lists the Louvre's top draws that must be included in your itinerary—absolutely no ifs, buts, and ands about it.

Musée Du Louvre

Amazing. Beautiful. Massive. Once the palace of ancient French kings, the Louvre now holds some of the world's finest pieces of art. I can't stress the popularity and significance of this museum enough. Many will say your Parisian vacation would not be complete without visiting this place. It's an absolute *must-see.*

The world-renowned art museum of the Louvre is nestled within the Right Bank in the 1st arrondissement where it doubles as a historic monument. In terms of number of visitors, the Louvre Museum is ranked 1st both nationally and globally. It houses some of the world's most ancient and significant archaeological finds along with the most celebrated masterpieces of the Italian Renaissance. Boasting over 35,000 exhibits, the sprawling Parisian landmark spans an area of 652,300 square feet. I recommend going to the Musée du Louvre during your first morning in Paris when your energy is at its peak. Trust me, you'll need it!

The entrance to the Louvre is nearly as famous as the museum itself. Designed by architect Ieoh Ming Pei in 1989, the Louvre entrance stands as a magnificent glass pyramid constructed from 675 panes of glass. Then there's the Medieval Louvre section which reveals the ancient foundations of the structure during its years as a royal palace. Medieval Louvre can be accessed through the Pyramid and descending the escalator to the Sully wing. The moat and ancient dungeons offer a glimpse into medieval times.

While there are thousands upon thousands of magnificent treasures at the Louvre, I've compiled a list of the top 10 works of arts that are not to be missed. That's not to say you shouldn't at least *try* to explore as much of the great masterpieces there. Your feet will probably be sore by the afternoon, but being able to say you've navigated a huge portion of the enormous museum is well worth the pain. Do it in the name of fine art!

1. *Mona Lisa* by **Leonardo da Vinci (Denon Wing, Room 6)**

You've seen her in pictures, in art books, and the internet. You, yourself, have pondered the mysteries surrounding her smile. Now you can see it in the flesh—or at least, the paper canvas. The most famous masterpiece ever painted is completely open for your viewing pleasure. Think you can unravel the mystery? Millions make the pilgrimage to the museum just to see the brush strokes of the *Mona Lisa*. If that doesn't take your breath away, I don't know what will.

Source: http://mentalfloss.com/article/62280/14-things-you-didnt-know-about-mona-lisa

2. *Nike of Samothrace* **(Denon Wing, Daru Staircase)**

Also known as "Winged Victory," this marble sculpture is a 2nd century work built in honor of the Greek goddess, Nike. Made of Parian marble, the sculpture conveys a sense of triumph and victorious glory from a battle in the sea. It's been prominently displayed at the Louvre since 1884. *Nike of Samothrace* is one of the most celebrated sculptures in the art world. ***Fun Fact***: The artist responsible for creating *Nike of Samothrace* intentionally left the right side of the statue plain since that was the side that would rarely be seen by viewers.

3. ***Raft of the Medusa* by Théodore Géricault (Denon wing, Room 77)**

An oversized oil painting by a French romantic painter, the *Raft of the Medusa* depicts a tragic moment in French history when the *Méduse* vessel sank off the coast of modern day Mauritania. Set adrift, the passengers of the *Méduse* fashioned a raft; all but 15 survived. The survivors resorted to cannibalism in the days before their rescue. Théodore Géricault was only 27 when he completed the Raft of the Medusa, his first major work.

Fun Fact: The *Raft of the Medusa* was painted in such a way that the viewer is drawn into the action as a participant. By setting up the stage of the painting in this way, Géricault ensured the empathetic response of viewers.

Source: http://michael-
shapcott.com/blog/tag/quote/

4. ***Psyche Revived by Cupid's Kiss*** **by**
   Antonio Canova
   (Richelieu Wing, Pavillon de Flore)

A deep, resonant name paired to a
sculpture that speaks volumes. *Psyche
Revived by Cupid's Kiss* is a perfect
rendition of true love. In 1793, Canova
used ethereal white marble in his
depiction of the mythical love story of the
god Cupid and his lover, Psyche. It depicts
Cupid at the height of love after awakening
Psyche with a passionate kiss. The
critically acclaimed sculpture is regarded
as a masterpiece – the quintessential
Neoclassical sculpture—and rightfully so.

5. *The Wedding Feast at Cana* by Paolo Veronese (Denon wing, Room 6)

This massive oil painting takes up an entire wall in the Louvre Museum from floor to ceiling. In fact, *Les Noces de Cana* is the biggest painting in the entire museum. Painted in 1553 in Venice, this magnificent composition depicts a miraculous story from the New Testament in which Jesus and his disciples attended a wedding celebration in Cana in the Galilee.

Cana is the setting in which Jesus' first miracle took place. According to the Gospel, Jesus turned water into wine towards the end of the wedding feast.

Fun Fact: Veronese's masterpiece is so large that Napoléon had to cut it in half in order to ship it from Italy to Paris in 1797. Upon arrival, the painting was stitched back together.

Source:
http://www.katapi.org.uk/Art/MarriageCana.ht
m

6. ***Vénus de Milo*** **by Alexandros of Antioch**
   (Sully Wing, Room 7)

Known as *Aphrodite of Milos* to some, *Vénus de Milo* is the highlight of the museum's antiquities department. Thought to have been created between 130 and 100 BCE, the statue is believed to depict the Greek goddess of love and beauty, Aphrodite. It's named after its place of discovery in the Greek island of Milos. No historian can say for sure what exactly the half-naked statue represents, but *Vénus de Milo* reflects the art of the late Hellenistic Period.

Fun Fact: Like many historical finds, *Vénus de Milo* is accompanied with its share of mysteries. The statue is widely renowned for the mystery surrounding her missing arms. Some theorists suggest that it was an apple she was holding in one hand while others strongly believe she held a mirror to revel in her beautiful reflection. Heck, historians aren't even entirely certain on the subject of the work. Some believe she's an entirely different goddess altogether—one that goes by name of Amphitrite.

Source:
https://www.tumblr.com/search/venus%20de%20 20milo%20olouvre

7. ***The Coronation of Napoléon* by Jacques-Louis David (Denon Wing, Room 75)**

Yet another immense oil painting on canvas, *Le Sacre de Napoléon*, as it's known in French, depicts the crowning of Napoléon at Notre-Dame de Paris. It was Napoléon I himself who commissioned the work in 1804 following his self-proclamation of Emperor. French painter, David, attended the coronation. In staying true to Napoléon's request, David depicted the ceremony in exact detail while adding glorification to the painting in order to appease the new Emperor of France.

Fun Fact: Napoléon actually crowned himself during his coronation instead of keeping with tradition by allowing the Pope to crown him. This was his way of making a statement about being the son of the Revolution and independence from the Church.

8. *The Lacemaker* by Jan Vermeer (Richelieu Wing, Room 38)

English for *La Dentellière, The Lacemaker* conforms to Vermeer's inclination towards painting scenes of everyday life. Though smaller than most, fellow painter and fan, Renoir, described *The Lacemaker* as the most beautiful painting in the world. Another famous painter, van Gogh, also praises *The Lacemaker* for its harmonious blend of colors, making it look more like an old photograph than an oil painting.

Symbolizing traditional feminine virtues, the painting depicts a young woman dressed in 1600s garb who is painstakingly working on her lacemaking. Vermeer has a unique painting style that entails a technique of blurring and emphasizing certain aspects. The result aims to mimic the human eye's natural optical field. This is why the central image is shown in sharp focus while the surroundings are slightly out of focus. It is thought that Vermeer left the wall behind the Dutch woman bare in order to eliminate any distractions from the central image.

Fun Fact: Measuring at 9.6 × 8.3 inches, *The Lacemaker* is Vermer's smallest work. At first glance, it really does appear to be a vintage photograph.

Source: https://vermeer0708.wordpress.com/the-lacemaker-1/

9. *The Seated Scribe* from Saqqara (Department of Egyptian Antiquities, Upper Floor)

Out of the 50,000 exhibits in the Louvre Egyptian antiquities department, *The Seated Scribe* is considered to be the most important work. Yet, we know neither his name, title, nor the time period during which he lived. Judging from his posture, kilt, and the fact that he holds a scroll signifies that the subject—whoever he may be—is, indeed, an Egyptian scribe.

What makes him so special is that he was sculpted extremely realistically, which demonstrates the high level of artistic éclat attained by ancient Egyptian artists. Stop by the Egyptian department at the Louvre to see the realistic sculpture for yourself.

Fun Fact: If you look closely, you'll see that the scribe's nipples are made up of a pair of wooden dowels. You might also notice that his right hand appears to be holding a missing brush—which would make sense, considering the scroll he holds with his left.

*Source:
https://www.pinterest.com/brennabrenana/art-history-chapter-3/*

10. **French Crown Jewels (Department of Decorative Arts)**

The French Crown Jewels offer a glimpse of the grandeur that once symbolized France's monarchy. Coronation crowns of old France were reflections of both the wealth and power of French kings. The key must-sees in this department include:

- ***Couronne de Louis XV***: This crown lies in Room 66 of the Denon Wing, and features two rows of pearls and eight perfect gems that alternate with pure diamonds.

- ***Diadème de la Duchesse d'Angoulème***: This is a dazzling tiara embellished with diamonds and emeralds.
- ***Couronne de l'Impératrice Eugénie***: This imperial crown is the most extravagant of the three. It is decorated with an astonishing 2,480 diamonds and 56 emeralds.

Source:
*https://www.flickr.com/photos/canadagood/340856611
7*

There is so much more to see in the Louvre Museum than can fit in this travel guide. Consider taking a guided "Masterpieces" tour for maximum insight into the Louvre's most prized artworks. Before you visit the museum, download the Louvre app as it's an extremely helpful guide.

The app includes audio-guided tours that allow visitors to navigate the museum at their own pace. It's a good idea to buy tickets in advance.

Remember to maximize the depth of your visit to the museum by focusing first on the key exhibits. It takes endurance to see all the highlights, so plan in advance and time the visit right.

Tuileries Garden

Just next door to the Musée du Louvre is the majestic wonder that is Jardin des Tuileries. Though small—covering only 2.5 acres of land— the garden is decorated with impressive sculptures and fountains of historical significance. With lovely terraces and well-kept ponds, the Tuileries Garden is the perfect setting for an afternoon stroll.

Source: http://raredelights.com/paris-endless-world-discover/tuileries-garden-5/

Place Vendôme

Near the Tuileries lies a perfectly proportioned plaza in the shape of an octagon. Surrounding Place Vendôme are beautiful private mansions, which are enough to bring out a gasp of awe. Once, a statue of Napoléon atop a 144-foot column stood in the plaza, but was destroyed in 1871 by a band of radicals. Today, Place Vendôme attracts millions of international tourists who come to the octagonal plaza just to witness its balance and proportion.

Fun Fact: No. 12 Place Vendôme was the home of the famous Polish composer, Chopin; he lived and died there. It was also the site where Napoléon III enjoyed scandalous trysts with his mistress.

Source: http://www.virtourist.com/europe/paris/27.htm

Musée De L'orangerie

While you're exploring the Tuileries Garden, don't forget to stop by Musée de l'Orangerie, the old greenhouse situated in the western end of the *jardin*. Within the sweeping galleries of this charming art museum, you'll find one of Monet's most famous works: *Water Lilies*.

Fun Fact: Monet planted water lilies in his

French garden prior to painting them, then spent the rest of his days capturing the image of the lilies. By the way, *Water Lilies* isn't just one painting: it's a series of masterpieces.

Source: http://en.parismuseumpass.com/musee-musee-national-de-l-orangerie-35.htm

Gallery Of Jeu De Paumme

The Tuileries Garden contains another small art gallery, this one centered around contemporary art. Within the Gallery of Jeu de Paumme, you'll find traditional photography showcased alongside both electronically and mechanically generated images.

Comédie-Française

Founded in 1680 and rebuilt in 1990, the Comédie-Française is one of the few state theaters in France. It's also the oldest theater group in the nation. Once housed in the Hôtel de

Guénégaud, the theater now occupies a spot on Place André-Malaux as part of the Palais Royal complex. After 400 years, the theater is still very much active and going strong.

Source: http://www.neoprofs.org/t11307-cherche-image-comedie-francaise

Palais-Royal

Hiding in the midst of the Louvre is the Royal Palace built by Cardinal Richelieu in 1629. The area around the palace is considered the quietest and most romantic public parks in France. Vibrant greenery, fountains, and century-old arcades make it an ideal setting for sweethearts who wish to relax throughout the afternoon. Even better, Palais-Royal is a one of the Parisian landmarks that can be visited free of charge. Dozens of 19th century shopping arcades line the garden, selling anything from trinkets to music boxes.

Fun Fact: Palais-Royal was never the residence of any king from the French Royal family.

Source: http://www.paris-architecture.info/PA-096.htm

Les Arts Décoratifs

Here is yet another museum that the Louvre area has to offer. It shares a wing with the Musée du Louvre, and promises to stir the design admirer hidden within you. Les Arts Décoratifs is comprised of three sub-museums laid out across nine floors. Many of the exhibits here are centered around decorative arts, graphics, and design. The museum is also home to an array of Renaissance furnishings, altarpieces plucked from the Middle Ages, and a collection of textiles. During your visit, don't forget to stop by the green velvet bed of the Parisian courtesan who inspired the boudoir in the novel *Nana*. Also, set aside a few minutes for the jewelry gallery on the second floor.

Place De La Concorde

While you're at the Louvre, stop by the site where 2,500 French people, including Marie Antoinette and Louis XVI lost their heads to the guillotine. The square lies at the foot of the Champs-Élysées. The centerpiece there is an absolute must-see: a colossal granite obelisk from the 8th century called the Luxor Obelisk that serves as a reminder of the friendship between France and Egypt during the 1800s.

Source: http://en.parisinfo.com/transport/90907/Place-de-la-Concorde

Saint-Eustache

The Catholic church of Saint-Eustache is a massive gothic structure that took a century to complete. It has been active for hundreds of years, and is still in use today. Situated at the entrance to Les Halles, Saint-Eustache was the top choice for baptisms, weddings, and funerals of ancient

Frenchmen.

Fun Fact: Saint-Eustache actively provides help and spiritual guidance for victims suffering from AIDS.

Nightlife

When the sun sets in Paris, the Parisian atmosphere becomes infused with upbeat conversation and clinking glasses. After a long day spent shopping and marveling over priceless masterpieces, you deserve to wind down at a hip Louvre bar. Here are a few options:

Ballroom Du Beef Club

If you're not paying extra attention, you might just miss the unmarked entrance to this popular cocktail bar. Ballroom du Beef Club is a classic example of a hole in the wall. The nondescript black door serving as the entrance to the bar tricks non-locals into a false sense of suspicion. In reality, Ballroom du Beef Club stands out with pressed tin ceilings and atmospheric lighting in a basement setting.

Bar D'art

If you've got a carefree, hipster demeanor, look no further for the ideal bar to let your hair down. Savor life with hip Parisians here and engage in intellectual conversation. Bar d'Art is the hippest spot in the Louvre. Alternative music and ambient lighting will put you in the right mood and a sense of relaxation.

Chacha Club

The Chacha Club is *the* place for the casual clubber. Inside, you'll find a multi-level space with a low-pressure 1930s vibe. A series of cozy rooms and countless corners offer tons of places conducive to friendly conversation. Check out the smoking lounge to get a glimpse of the cool cats of the city. Make a friend, and pass the night away here with delicious non-virgin concoctions and traditional French food.

Jefrey's

If you're looking for a more intimate, quiet club atmosphere, Jefrey's is the club for you. Relax on loveseats with a unique cocktail blend and let the DJ's select tracks speak to your soul. Expect to cross paths with stylish Parisians offering good company. One awesome aspect of Jefrey's allows you to order a bottle, and if you don't get the time to finish, they'll actually put your name on the bottle and store it for next time. It must be the chic surroundings, because for some reason, Jefrey's *knows* that you'll be coming back for more.

Kong

If you love to dance and aren't afraid of a little rowdiness, Kong is an eccentric little nightclub that offers panoramic views of the Paris skyline. It infuses a mixture of French and Japanese culture Clink glasses over a plate of dim sum with Parisian regulars as you showcase your best dance moves to the hopping house music.

Chapter 3: Your Guide to the Champs-Élysées

Champs-Élysées has upheld its position as the most popular avenue in France—and, quite possibly, in the whole of Europe. Equivalent to New York's Times Square in scope and extravagance, Champs-Élysées is one of the few places in Paris where French elegance meets frugality. Here you'll find a McDonald's amidst three-star joints, a clear demonstration of the integration in Champs-Élysées. Whether you have hauteur or economical tastes, there's a shop, hotel, and restaurant on the avenue that's right for you.

Must-Sees on Champs-Élysées

Arc De Triomphe

At Place Charles de Gaulle at the western end of Champs-Élysées stands the world's most monumental triumphal arc. Arc de Triomphe is the most famous monument in Paris, and is France's pride and joy. The massive structure clocks in at 164 feet high, 148 feet wide, and 72 feet deep. Commissioned in 1806 in honor of the French soldiers who fought in the Napoléonic wars, Arc de Triomphe sets the tone for public monuments with patriotic messages. The names of heroes and generals are engraved within the arch. A tomb of an unknown soldier of WWI also lies beneath the arch.

Fun Fact: The Arc de Triomphe was commissioned in 1806 by Napoléon, but he never got to see the finished product.

Source: http://lifewallpaperz.com/cat/20/arc-de-triomphe-03.html

Grand Palais

At the other end of Champs-Élysées stands the exquisite Grand Palais which hosts large-scale art exhibitions. The stone edifice was built in 1897 in the style of Beaux-Arts architecture which is characterized by ornate decoration. The curved-glass roof and elaborate ornamentations of the Grand Palais sets a fitting tone for hosting annual Chanel fashion shows. Over 1.5 million visitors flock to Grand Palais every year to watch the many shows staged there, from cars to jewelry to haute couture.

These shows are the hottest tickets in town, so skip the long queue and book your ticket in an advance.

Source: http://viceversahotel.com/blog/grand-palais-paris/

Petit Palais

Right across from Grand Palais stands its smaller, sister palace that showcases a small collection of artwork by the likes of Monet, Courbet, and other notable French artists. Most art shows here are free; that's not to say any of the exhibitions are lacking in excellence. Beyond its stone façade is an exquisite architectural marvel of glass and marble. Large windows in the main galleries offer panoramic views of the Seine River. Take selfies with the busts of sixteen famous artists, then head out to the garden café and have a stress-free lunch on the quiet terrace.

Fun Fact: Both Grand and Petit Palais were built for the World Fair, and were meant to be temporary structures.

Source: http://www.petitpalais.paris.fr/en/le-petit-palais/building-history-and-interior-decoration

Cité De L'architecture Et Du Patrimoine

Located in Palais de Chaillot, this gem of French architecture is the largest architectural museum in the world. Its main exhibit, the Musée des Monuments Français, contains three permanent galleries spread out over 86,000 square feet:

- **Galerie des Moulages**: This gallery contains 350 plaster casts of original French architecture pieces from the 12th to 18th centuries. Though these exhibits are only reproductions, they are, by no means, ordinary.

- **Galerie Moderne et Contemporaine**: This gallery showcases outstanding French architecture from the 1850s to the present, including international works.

- **Galerie des Peintures Murales et des Vitraux**: Also a gallery filled with reproductions, this one exhibits extraordinary wall paintings and stained-glass windows from historic monuments.

Musée National De La Marine

Also located in Palais de Chaillot, this maritime museum consists of a permanent collection going back to Louis XV's reign. The naval museum contains must-see ancient weapons, a statue of the sea god, Neptune, the galleys of Louis XVI, and imperial barges once belonging to Napoléon I. Over 300 years of maritime history and technological advances are displayed here. You can even catch a glimpse of the living conditions onboard Louis XVI's ships.

Source: http://www.musee-marine.fr/musee-national-de-la-marine-toulo

Palais Galliera

Inside the stylish mansion that is Palais Galliera lies the city's Museum of Fashion. Whether you're a devoted fashion buff or you're simply curious about the history of French fashion, Palais Galliera should not be missed. The museum houses over 70,000 fashion-related items dating back hundreds of centuries. At Palais Galliera, you can compare old French fashion design with fashion of the current era. Expect to see actual 18th century costumes worn by historical French people like Marie Antoinette and Louis XVII, as well as relatively modern pieces worn by famous actresses like Audrey Hepburn. In addition to costumes, Palais Galliera also features early designs by Balenciaga, Yves Saint Laurent, Christian Dior, and Givenchy.

Musée D'art Moderne De La Ville De Paris

Often undervalued, this low-traffic museum of contemporary art showcases temporary exhibitions of art from the 20th century. The lower floor is reserved for permanent exhibitions featuring Fauvist artworks and Pablo Picasso's paintings created when he was only just experimenting in Cubism. Visiting Musée d'Art Moderne de la Ville de Paris is a pleasant experience free of long queues as it draws fewer crowds.

Aquarium De Paris

If you're looking for a little time-out from history, opt for a fun-filled zoo adventure at France's all-time favorite aquarium. This aquatic zoo isn't just for kids; there's plenty of fun to be had for adults, too. Aside from contemporary aquariums filled with hundreds of species of sea life, Aquarium de Paris contains two large cinemas and a fish-touch pool.

Source: http://www.parisselectbook.com/en/aquarium-de-paris-happily-wiggles/

Nightlife

Once you've finished exploring the sights on Champs-Élysées, go barhopping! If you're not too tired, that is. Champs-Élysées is hands down the best place in Paris to barhop due to the affordability of most of the bars there.

Crazy Horse

If you're not afraid of a little fun, stop by one of Paris' better cabaret bars for the ultimate cabaret experiences. Founded in 1951, Crazy Horse is famous among Parisians for their beautiful dancers decked out in Louboutin and artsy stripteases. The famous burlesque dancer, Dita von Teese, once performed at Crazy Horse.

Buddha Bar

If plan on spending a night in a chic hotel on Champs-Élysées, then you may as we explore a handful of bars and dance clubs. Once you've gotten your cabaret fix, head on over to nearby Buddha Bar to drink away the blush from Crazy Horse. The bar is replete with huge palm fronds, red satin walls, and a colossal statue of Buddha that holds court over the bar. Grab a bite of pan-Asian fare, mingle, and move on to the next bar! By the way, don't party too hard: you'll need your energy for the next bar—trust me.

Black Calavados

The sleek nightclub known as Black Calvados is a favorite hangout among Parisian trendsetters. This is a place you'll want to splurge a little in. It's the perfect cherry on top during your stay at Champs-Élysées. Here, the party starts fashionably late—midnight—so it gives you time to enjoy Crazy Horse and Buddha Bar beforehand. Make sure you're dressed to the nines just in case you bump elbows with a local celebrity. Once inside, order a Black Kiss shot and dance the night away.

Chapter 4: Relaxing at the Eiffel Tower

It wouldn't hurt to break away from the nightlife and French history for half a day to recharge at the most famous landmark in Europe. Here lies the cultural icon of France and the most romantic spots in the world. When it was erected in 1889, the Eiffel Tower surpassed the Washington Monument as the tallest man-made structure in the world. Standing at 1,063 feet tall, its height is equivalent to an 81-story skyscraper. The Eiffel Tower held the title as tallest structure in the world until 1930 when the Chrysler Building in New York City was built. Today, the Eiffel Tower stands as the crown jewel of Paris and France's pride and joy. It's the most visited monument in the world.

The first two levels of the Eiffel Tower can be accessed by ascending the stairs, and contains a number of restaurants. The observatory on the third level is typically accessed via elevators. The highest you can go is 906 feet, which is still high enough to cause vertigo. Here at the highest publically-accessed platform of the beloved iron tower, you'll be able to see the entire city for miles. This is the site of thousands of romantic moments and marriage proposals from visitors all over the world. Make the most of your visit to the Eiffel Tower by exploring some of the other landmarks in the area.

Fun Fact: Technically, the Eiffel Tower is still the tallest man-made building in the world. The aerial addition to the top of the tower makes the Eiffel Tower taller than the Chrysler Building by 17 feet.

Source: http://www.wsj.com/articles/eiffel-tower-closed-as-staff-stage-strike-1432303459

Sights

The area surrounding the Eiffel Tower consists of several other tourist attractions.

Champ De Mars

Champ de Mars is a long expanse of grass that leads up to the Eiffel Tower. Flanked by tree-lined paths, it once served as the site of the World Fair back in the late 1800s. The landscaped park is now an ideal setting for afternoon picnics, a friendly game of soccer or Frisbee, and outdoor concerts. Bastille Day fireworks draws millions of visitors, but on any other ordinary day, you'll find people sprawled out on the grass just letting off steam.

Source: http://www.discoverwalks.com/blog/free-things-to-do-in-paris/

Les Égouts

Les Égouts translates to "The Sewers," but before you judge, try to keep an open mind. After all, your Paris vacation wouldn't really be complete without a little adventure thrown in for fun. The 1,650 foot stretch of tunnels that make up Les Égouts serve as an exhibit that offers a glimpse into the underbelly of Paris. Visitors can actually roam the tunnels beneath Paris via walkways. The walls are embellished here and there with photos accompanied with English explanations that clarify the inner workings of the sewer system. People who have already navigated through the sewers swear it doesn't smell. Les Égouts may be a little grimy, but it's definitely not squalid.

Fun Fact: The tunnels beneath Paris are wide enough for a whole barge to go through.

Source: http://www.20minutes.fr/planete/393190 20100324-rue-a-nature-trajet-eaux-usees-parisiennes

Hôtel Des Invalides

This Baroque complex doesn't only stand out due to its magnificent golden dome: Hôtel des Invalides also contains the tomb of the mean old French dictator Napoléon Bonaparte. It wasn't always his final resting place though; he died in 1821, but his remains weren't moved here until 1840. Initially, the facility was built for the sole purpose of housing disabled soldiers in 1670. At its peak, there were over 4,000 veterans residing beneath the towering golden dome. Here you'll also find the Musée de l'Armee which exhibits thousands of military armor and weapons. The rear of the complex consists of an old church called Église du Dome—a sight you should definitely check out.

Fun Fact: Napoléon's sarcophagus is actually six

separate coffins that works almost like a Russian nesting doll. The visible sarcophagus is made up of red quartzite which is encircled by statues that symbolize the dictator's campaigns of conquest. The weapons museum at Hôtel des Invalides contains some of Napoléon's personal belongings, including his trademark gray frock and bicorne hat.

Source: http://www.hotels-paris-france-hotels.com/hotel-des-invalides/

Palais Bourbon

You're probably well aware by now that Paris is rife with palaces, so it doesn't come as a surprise that there would be a palace sharing grass with Napoléon's tomb and an ancient weapons gallery. The French Parliament has called Palais Bourbon home since 1798. Its construction was ordered by Napoléon who was very specific on the building's architectural requirements. He demanded that the façade should be colonnaded in order to equal that of the Madeleine, a Parisian church.

Inside, there is a massive library with cupolas painted by French artist, Eugène Delacroix. Touring Palais Bourbon is free, but spots are in short supply so be sure to make reservations. Security is tight here, so make sure you have your passport on hand.

Source:
http://www.snipview.com/q/Nearby:_Palais_Bourbon

Musée Du Quai Branly

So many museums, so little time. This museum, however, is one you should definitely make time for while you're in the area. Built by acclaimed architect, Jean Nouvel, this spectacular museum overlooks the Seine River and contains nearly half a million doodads plucked from a variety of cultures outside of Europe. Only about 3,500 of these are currently exhibited to the public, but the museum is still worth a look. The exhibits that *are* featured consist of indigenous art from Africa, Asia, the Americas, and Oceania. From funeral masks to shaman drums, to Asian textiles and African statues, there's something here that appeals to every visitor.

Before you leave, head upstairs and grab a bite to eat at Les Ombres on the fifth floor. The trendy restaurant is on the costly end of the price spectrum, but not to worry! There's a more affordable restaurant on the ground floor called Le Café Branly that ensures the budget-conscious don't go hungry.

Fun Fact: Musée du quai Branly is hard to miss due to the living wall of exotic plants that surround the museum like a fence.

There isn't a big party scene in the area near the Eiffel Tower, which is why it's the perfect place to recharge and get your energy levels back up. But that's not to say you can't unwind with a nightcap at one of the two dozen hotels within walking distance of the Eiffel Tower. Some of the more affordable hotels include Grand Hôtel Lévêque nestled among casual cafés and the even cheaper—but charming—Hôtel du Champ de Mars which offers picturesque views and cozy rooms.

Chapter 5: Exploring Les Grands Boulevards

Once you've sufficiently recharged, head over to Les Grands Boulevards for an entire day of fun and adventure. Beautifully tree-lined and comprised of a series of boulevards, the area forms a significant part of the urban landscape of Paris. Dotting the avenues are countless Parisian street vendors, fast-food joints, and chain stores. Parisians associate leisure with the boulevards, thus, you'll find plenty of impeccably-dressed locals promenading down the avenues. Many agree that Les Grands Boulevards are the best streets in Paris.

Fun Fact: It's not entirely clearly *which* of the Parisian boulevards in the area are classed under the Grands Boulevards, even among locals born and raised there.

Must-Sees and Must-Dos

Aside from the many department stores providing an endless amount of shopping, Les Grands Boulevards are also a cultural destination that plays home to dozens of famous landmarks. Realistically speaking, you won't be able to hit all the sights in the neighborhood, so I've compiled a list of the best of the best that the Grand Boulevards have to offer.

Opéra Garnier

Also known as Palais Garnier, this 2,000-seat opera house continues to uphold its title as the most famous in the world. Built in the Beaux-Arts and Second Empire architectural style and boasting gold leaf and colored marble, the structure itself is a tourist attraction. In fact, Opéra Garnier is so lavish, so absurdly luxurious, that it once generated bad criticism from those who frowned upon unnecessary overspending and public displays of extravagance. The opera house goes beyond vocabulary in scope and beauty. See it for yourself; Opèra Garnier promises to make jaws drop each and every time.

Fun Fact: Opéra Garnier formed the setting for Gaston Leroux's 1910 novel, *The Phantom of the Opera*, which would later become a popular musical.

Source:
http://www.aviewoncities.com/paris/operagarnier.htm

Musée Jacquemart-André

Here is yet another opulent museum of Paris whose story attracts international visitors by the thousands. While small, Musée Jacquemart-Andre boasts a large collection of art and furnishings assembled by a 19th century husband-and-wife duo who shared a love of art. Edouard André, a banking magnate, and his artist wife, Nélie Jacquemart, often traveled on passion-fueled journeys to Italy in search of all the artworks from the Renaissance that they could get their hands on. The pair amassed a vast collection of art from the Italian Renaissance era as well as French masterpieces. The best time to visit this museum is on an early Sunday morning. That way, you are more likely to avoid the queues and able to enjoy brunch at the café before moving on.

Le Musée Gourmand Du Chocolat

Prepare to embark on a journey through a very different kind of history. You've heard of chocolate factories, but a chocolate *museum*? It's not every day you come across a museum dedicated to chocolate, so Le Musée Gourmand du Chocolat is a pleasant surprise that awaits you on the Grand Boulevards of Paris. The hundreds of chocolate-related exhibits here are spread over three floors. Included in the collection are artifacts tracing back to ancient Mayan, Spanish, and Aztec civilizations, including terra cotta dishes and old porcelain pots used in making and storing chocolate. A tour through the museum usually finishes with a bang—a chocolate-making demo with a free tasting session.

Musée De La Vie Romantique

Translated to the Museum of the Romantic Life, visiting this historic place is like being teleported from the big city to the distant French countryside. The museum is housed inside a rustic 1830s mansion bundled within a gorgeous tree-lined, paved courtyard. Drawings by French artists like Delacroix comprise a large portion of the museum's small collection. Among the unique exhibits featured here, you'll find a mold of Chopin's hand.

The star of the collection, however, is the collective memorabilia of George Sand. The French novelist was famous for her publicized romantic affairs with various notable artists of

Paris, which influenced the erection of the museum. Her jewelry is showcased in several display cases. Once you've marveled at her extravagant bejeweled pieces, head outside and enjoy an afternoon tea in the charming garden.

Fun Fact: George Sand and Frédéric Chopin were lovers for years.

Source: http://parismusees.paris.fr/en/museum-romantics

Musée National Gustave-Moreau

Gustave Moreau was a highly distinguished French Symbolist artist who painted biblical-themed watercolors and created sculptures of mythological creatures. What was once his townhome is now a charming little art museum that showcases some of his best works, including *Jacob and the Angel*, *The Apparition*, and *Jupiter and Semele*. Here there are no blank spaces on the walls.

Passage Des Panoramas

Finally, a bazaar to wrap up your day on Les Grands Boulevards! And not just your normal bazaar: Passage des Panoramas is a food-lover's paradise. Opened in the 1830s, the large arcade is Paris' oldest covered passages. An exploration of Passage des Panoramas brings you to high quality bars, five gourmet restaurant chains, vintage boutiques, and charming stamp and postcard shops.

Source: http://en.parisinfo.com/paris-museum-monument/100264/Passage-des-Panoramas

Party in Style on Les Grands Boulevards

As with all popular boulevards, the Grand Boulevards of Paris offers ample crowd-pleasing nightclub options. To Parisians, the adult playparks on Les Grand Boulevards is the place to see and be seen.

Barramundi

Dim, golden-hued lighting, tropical beverages, great food, friendly people, trendy surroundings—what more could you ask for of a bar lounge? Barramundi mostly attracts sophisticated partiers—if ever there were any—in search of an elegant night out. If that description suits your style, Barramundi is the best option for you.

Corcoran's Irish Pub

"He who opens his mouth most is the one who opens his purse least." That's just one of many witty quotes plastered on the walls of this traditional Irish pub. A perfect solution after a long, hot trip through Les Grands Boulevards, Corcoran's Irish Pub offers an ample drink menu and eye-catching bar. As night falls, chummy conversation gives way to dancing and raucous laughter.

Source: http://www.guideparisci.com/delaville-cafe/

If you happen to be in the mood for drinking in a Baroque-style nightclub setting, head over to Delaville Café over on Bonne Nouvelle. The café's huge sidewalk terrace makes it an unmissable stop on the Grand Boulevards. Once a 19th century brothel, Delaville Café still retains a hefty dose of glitz and glamour. Rococo features can still be seen throughout, and the building is now frequented by chic Parisians.

Chapter 6: A Fun Latin Quarter Adventure

Imagine a Parisian version of the college town of Gainesville, Florida. The Latin Quarter is ground zero for students, and has been for over 800 years. When the first French university, La Sorbonne, was erected here, students from all over Europe flocked to the neighborhood. The Latin Quarter is so named because students were predominantly Latin-speaking. Over the centuries, the neighborhood evolved from a student community to a local hotspot thanks to the hefty amount of shops, quaint cafés, and bars.

On Boulevard Saint-Michel, the main street that runs through the neighborhood, you'll find a fairly equal local-to-tourist ratio wandering along. Straying away from the busy thoroughfare will take you to cute little side streets where quiet bistros and charming boutiques are sprinkled here and there.

Touristy Things to Do

Aside from cheap, hassle-free shopping and mellow eateries, there are dozens of activities to get into while you're in the Latin Quarter. Below lists the top tourist favorites.

Panthéon

The Panthéon is to Paris as St. Peter's is to Rome. It's one of the earliest examples of the Neoclassism architectural style. Built in the 1700s by architect, Jacques-Germain Soufflot, and originally served as a church to house the relics of St. Genevieve, the patron saint of Paris. Today, the Panthéon functions as a national mausoleum containing the remains of distinguished French figures, including Dumas, Voltaire, Victor Hugo, and Marie Curie. The Panthéon's gigantic dome is a must-see, but won't be open to the public until late 2015 due to a major restoration. The crypt and nave, however, are both very much accessible.

Source:
http://esclh.blogspot.com.au/2015/06/workshop-french-association-of-young.html

Arènes De Lutèce

Admittedly, Paris isn't the first city that comes to mind when you're looking for an archaeological ruins to explore. By now, though, we already know that Paris is full of surprises. You may remember from Chapter 1 that old Paris was once a Roman city called Lutetia, and that the ancient Romans who settled in the city built a huge amphitheater. That very amphitheater still lies in Paris—in the Latin Quarter, in fact. And it's open for exploration!

If you have a penchant for adventure, then the Lutetia Amphitheatre should be your first stop as soon as you arrive in the Latin Quarter. Completed in the 1st century AD, the circular open-air venue was once a site for gladiatorial combats. Think Colosseum in Rome, but on a smaller, simpler scale. Arènes de Lutèce could sit 15,000 people back when it was still standing. It's considered the most important remains from the Gallo-Roman era in France.

Source: http://www.coolstuffinparis.com/les-arenes-de-lutece.php

Jardin Des Plantes

After a hot day at the ruins of the Lutetia Amphitheatre, cool off at the botanical gardens in the heart of the neighborhood. Have a quick power lunch at one of three kiosk cafés here. The rose garden and soaring greenhouses are not to be missed. Plant lovers will enjoy the wide array of tropical and exotic plants housed in Jardin des Plantes.

Source: http://www.shopbird.com/blog/2013/04/april-in-paris/

Grande Galerie De L'evolution

Here is a four-story natural history museum situated in the Jardin des Plantes where biology buffs unite. The vast 19th century metal-and-glass science hall is equipped with over 7,000 preserved specimens ranging in diversity, from taxidermied little beetles to animals as big as an elephant. One of the highlights of the museum is the humungous skeleton of a blue whale. Another is a taxidermied rhinoceros which was actually

Louis XV's royal pet once upon a time. Both adults and children will enjoy one of the newer additions to the museum: an amazing color-changing ceiling that replicates twilight, storm clouds, and even the scorching Savannah sun.

Source: http://www.mnhn.fr/fr/visitez/lieux/grande-galerie-evolution

Le Grande Mosquée De Paris

The Grand Mosque of Paris is an immaculate white edifice with a 108-foot minaret. It was built in 1926 as a token of gratitude to the Muslim soldiers who helped defend France against German troops during WWI. While the prayer rooms in the mosque aren't open to the public, the structure itself is awe-inspiring. There's still plenty of things to do there, like get an Turkish massage, enjoy a cup of mint tea at the onsite café, or sink your teeth into a delicious plate of couscous at the restaurant

Rue Mouffetard

Sure, Rue Mouffetard is but a crooked street, but there's so much significance to it. Not only is the cobblestone street nearly as old as Paris itself, it was also a Roman road that led from then Lutetia to Italy, the ancient Romans' country of origin. The best feature of Rue Mouffetard is the portion of street where shops and cafés abound. This area combines simplicity and luxury, offering everything from gourmet cheeses to fine wines to roast chicken.

Saint-Julien-Le-Pauvre

Holding the title for one of the three oldest religious buildings in Paris, this tiny shrine was founded nearly a millennium ago in 1045. Back in those days, the Romanesque-style church served as a rendezvous spot for university students attending La Sorbonne. During Dante's time, he regularly attended mass at Saint-Julien-le-Pauvre while he was writing the *Divine Comedy*. While inside, keep your eyes peeled for original pillars which are etched with carvings of demons. After a good walkthrough, head out to the garden and relax on a bench to savor the breathtaking view of Notre-Dame.

Saint-Étienne-Du-Mont

Yet another spectacular church, Saint-Étienne-du-Mont was once the burial site of St. Geneviève. Many Popes of the past have visited this religious shrine to pay homage to the patron saint. The church is unique owing to its eclectic architectural style which draws features from Renaissance, Gothic, and Baroque elements.

Most French churches were built in the Gothic style. Keep an eye out for the marker on the floor near the entrance that signifies the exact area where a Parisian archbishop was stabbed to death in 1857.

Source:http://www.wsj.com/articles/SB1000142405270
23046928045772854539460525o4

Clink Glasses with European Students

As with all college towns, the Latin Quarter also

offers a selection of clubs and pubs for those in need of a nightcap or two. Since it's a relatively small town, the nightlife here doesn't have a big-city vibe. There are only a handful of pubs, including Polly Maggoo and Delmas, both teeming with students. One major cabaret dominates the neighborhood called Paradis Latin which amazes and astounds with incredible acrobatics and eye-popping light shows. Curio Parlor is one option if you're in the mood for dancing amidst a library-like room with exposed brick walls.

Chapter 7: From Montmartre to Montparnasse

As their name suggests, both Montmartre and Montparnasse are Parisian hills. Exploring both areas can be squeezed into one whole day of fun-filled Parisian cheer.

Montmartre

The cobbled alleys of this Parisian hill lend a village-like feel to the area. Wandering off the beaten path will lead you to this large hill in the 18th arrondissement. Montmartre is so charming—not to mention, free—that it's well worth a trip, especially if you want 360° views of Paris without having to pay to climb the Eiffel Tower. Free skyline views are what makes thousands of visitors gravitate to the top of Montmartre.

The summit of Montmartre is the highest point in Paris. Already a 426-footer, the hill is further heightened by the dominating structure that is the Basilica of the Sacré Cœur—Montmartre's crown jewel. Don't be fooled by the hamlet feel of the town, though: Montmartre is known as a nightclub district. But that's for later. First and foremost: the top-rated sights.

Fun Fact: It's widely believed that the top of

Montmartre was a sacred site where Druids were worshipped.

Source: http://www.aparisguide.com/montmartre

Sacré-Cœur

We begin with the obvious: Sacred Heart Basilica, the highlight of Montmartre and the epitome of the term, "castle in the sky." Yes, Sacré-Cœur is a dream. Both locals and tourists swear that visiting the beautiful basilica is the closest real-world stairway-to-heaven experience. Construction began in 1875 and finished in 1914. Yes, it took 49 years to build Sacré-Cœur. It was only consecrated in 1919 following the end of WWI.

If you're up for a climb, I highly recommend ascending the spiral staircase to the top of the basilica's dome. This point offers the best visual treat in the whole church. Another amazing sight lies within Sacré-Cœur—a gigantic mosaic set high above the choir where it remains as one of the world's largest mosaics. Named *Christ in Majesty* by its creator, Luc-Olivier Merson, the golden mosaic depicts Jesus with a gilded heart, surrounded by a number of figures including the Virgin Mary and Joan of Arc. Expect to gape in awe at the stained glass windows, countless vaulted arches, and the portico's bronze doors, which are adorned with various biblical scenes.

Source:
http://www.gothereguide.com/sacre+coeur+paris-place/

Halle Saint-Pierre

At the foot of Sacré-Cœur, you'll find a 19th century market built from iron and glass. The market hall exhibits folk art pieces by international artists—must-sees if you're a raw art buff. Inside, you'll also come across a bookstore, as well as a nice little café that serves quiches and homemade desserts.

Source: http://www.cityzeum.com/halle-saint-pierre

Moulin Rouge

Everyone who's anyone knows what Moulin Rouge showcases: naughty performances by beautiful cabaret dancers. Now you can see the world-famous cabaret for yourself. When it opened in 1889, Moulin Rouge quickly became a hotspot for aristocrats and French professionals. Cabarets are the equivalent of American gentleman's clubs whose members consist of wealthy businessmen. Whatever you plan on doing at Moulin Rouge is up to you—just don't forget to stop by the Moulin Rouge gift shop on your way out.

Source:
http://www.pariscityvision.com/en/pariscitytourmoulin rouge

Musée De L'érotisme

In the home of Moulin Rouge, it's only fitting that there's a museum dedicated to erotic art. Montmartre is, after all, Paris' red light district. At the museum, you'll find a collection of erotic world art along with racy cartoons and photographs of French prostitutes—if you're of age, that is.

Carré Roland Dorgelès

Stepping foot on Carré Roland Dorgelès is like a blast from the past. Probably the most peaceful section of Montmartre, this quiet square offers a glimpse into the neighborhood when it was just an off-the-radar provincial village. Named after French novelist, Roland Dorgelès, the cobblestoned square is shaded by hundred-year-old trees, providing an ideal setting for an afternoon walk. Back in the day, this area of Montmartre was a gathering site between avant-garde artists and writers sharing inspiration. As you wander down the cobblestone streets here, remember that you are walking on the very ground where artists like Picasso, Max Jacob, and Modigliani once frequented.

Place Du Tertre

Place du Tertre is the center of Montmartre's art scene. Jam-packed with multicolored artists' stalls, this small cobblestone plaza offers a picturesque setting perfect for whiling away the afternoon. Plenty of benches are provided to allow you to soak up the beautiful scene. The many portraitists and caricaturists that set up shop in Place du Tertre brings the many tourists in Montmartre to the square in search of souvenirs. Have a crepe at one of the stands, enjoy an afternoon tea, or bust out your Nikon and take dozens of pictures in front of the many handsome 18th century buildings.

Eglise Saint-Pierre De Montmartre

Just a few steps away from Place du Tertre, you'll come across the relics of a Benedictine Abbey dating back to the 12th century. The church's history, however, goes back further by several hundred years, during a time when it was an ancient Roman temple devoted to Mercury. Inside the church, you'll find vestiges of the 7th century, including a set of well-preserved black marble columns.

Musée Du Montmartre

A short walk from the Church of Saint-Pierre brings you to a gorgeous 17th century mansion that houses a museum dedicated to the history of Montmartre. Discover Montmartre's early years and the evolution of the creativity that the place now effuses. Among the museum's prized collections are paintings, posters, manuscripts, books, and photos that depict Montmartre's colorful history.

Espace Dalí

Salvador Dalí, Spanish artist, leader of the Surrealist movement, and creator of unusual artworks, is celebrated highly enough to warrant an entire museum dedicated to his work. Espace Dalí allows visitors to access the wonderful, yet curious world of Dalí. Many of his paintings bore odd titles such as *Dream Caused by the Flight of a Bee Around a Pomegranate a Second Before Awakening, Swans Reflecting Elephants*, and *Apparition of Face and Fruit Dish on a Beach*. You may be laughing now, but coming face-to-face with Dalí's masterpieces will leave you awe-inspired.

Source:
http://www.francetravelthemes.pro/en/47/espace-dali/
When the sun sets in Montmartre and school is out, there's only one thing left to do: party! As promised, here are some of the most popular nightclubs in the city's red light district:

Chez Moune

Once a lesbian cabaret, Chez Moune dance club now attracts young hipsters of both genders. Set in a basement underground, Chez Moune plays an eclectic mix of techno and electro-rock. And the best part about it? There's no cover! And free entry means packed dance floors and a supercharged atmosphere.

Source: *http://www.cool-cities.com/chez-*

moune-822/

Au Lapin Agile

Here's an authentic cabaret that from the mid-1800s that's still opened today. You won't find any topless dancers here; Au Lapin Agile prides itself on being a relatively modest cabaret that features live music and poetry. At one point, it was a popular hangout for struggling artists like Modigliani and Picasso who often traded their paintings for meals.

Fun Fact: The famous Montmartre cabaret was originally called Cabaret des Assassins. According to tradition, a band of assassins broke and murdered the owner's son.

Source: *http://www.au-lapin-agile.com/*

Café La Fuormi

French for "The Ant," La Fuormi teems with pretty Parisian girls in skimpy outfits, which makes it a popular hangout for the guys. Party with the cool kids of Montmartre where inside, a funky bar-slash-café awaits you.

Dirty Dick

Don't be fooled by the name of this pub: Dirty Dick is actually a trendy Polynesian beach hut. Here, you might find yourself lounging on rattan chairs, sipping tropical drinks, or laughing with locals around a punchbowl called "Amazombie." Once you party at Dirty Dick, you'll never look at tiki lounges in the same light again.

Michou

Yet another well-known cabaret, Michou puts on a spectacular and humorous performance entailing men dressed in drag. It's a great place to let loose and cool off after a hot climb to the top of Montmarte. The owner, Michou, is usually there and he's hard to miss seeing as he's always decked out in blue.

Glass

The dark, candlelit space in Glass is a haunt among sophisticated hipsters. At the bar, you'll find a frozen drinks machine that dispenses margaritas. Here, there's a huge drink menu and gourmet hot dogs. Glass is also the only place in Paris where you'll find a boilermaker—a shot of whiskey chased by a glass of beer.

Montparnasse

Located on the Left Bank, Montparnasse is less of a hill and more like a flattened, slightly upraised geographical quirk. Back in Paris' early years, Montparnasse was a hilly area. As the city grew more and more prosperous, the hill was leveled, giving way to tall building and a train station. Montparnasse got its name from the 17th century students who came to the hill to recite poetry and nicknamed the place after "Mount Parnassus," a mountain of Greek mythology. Today, Montparnasse offers moderately priced cafés, reasonable rents, and a real Parisian vibe that's not as trendy as the neighborhoods on the Right Bank.

Tour Montparnasse

The 17th tallest building in the European Union, Tour Montparnasse, is a 689-foot office building comprised of 59 floors. When it was constructed in the 1970s, it was the tallest skyscraper in France until it was surpassed by Tour First in 2011. The tower's large proportions were criticized during its early years, with many stating the skyscraper was out of place in Paris' urban landscape. The lack of windows gives the skyscraper an intimidating quality.

It has been said that climbing to the top of the tower was worthwhile owing to the fact that it was the only place from which the tower couldn't be seen. If you've got the time, by all means, go visit the second ugliest building in the world, as rated by a 2008 poll of editors. While the building isn't as awe-inspiring as other skyscrapers of the world, the view from the observation deck on the 56th floor is amazing. The top floor consists of a roof terrace that is open to visitors, accessible by climbing another three flights from the observation deck.

Source: http://www.telerama.fr/monde/la-tour-

Cimetière Du Montparnasse

This 47-acre non-denominational cemetery is the final resting place of countless illustrious residents of Montparnasse. A few notable interments here include Guy de Maupassant, Alfred Dreyfus, poet Charles Baudelaire, and Frédéric Bartholdi, the architect who designed the Statue of Liberty. Once an ancient farmland, the picturesque cemetery opened in 1824 and is the second largest burial ground in the city.

Fondation Cartier Pour L'art Contemporain

On Boulevard Raspail in the Montparnasse quarter, you'll find yet another French museum of contemporary art. Founded in 1984, the glass structure is a relatively new non-profit museum featuring   art exhibits by many established artists from all over the world—approximately 1,000 works by 300 artists. The Fondation Cartier also gives young, struggling artists a chance to debut their work and offers both family tours and creative workshops for aspiring artists. The center is surrounded by a beautifully landscaped woodland garden. Try to go on a Thursday evening when the museum hosts Nomadic Nights featuring dance, film, fashion, and music. Advanced tickets are available on the museum's website.

Jardin Atlantique

There is no shortage of landscaped gardens in Paris. The public park and garden is situated on the large roof covering the tracks of the Gare Montparnasse railway station. Here, you can actually hear the announcement of train departures through the ventilatoe shafts placed around the garden. Nestled among modernistic glass-and-steel buildings, Jardin Atlantique is rife with a large assortment of plant life typically found in coastal regions near the Atlantic—hence, the garden's name.

While you're in the area, check out the two museums in the 8.4-acre garden:

1. **Mémorial du Maréchal-Leclerc**: Small, but highly informative, this museum is perfect for history buffs—particularly those interested in WWII history. The displays and exhibits here are well laid out and descriptions are written in English. If you take the time to read the placards in full, you'll be able to catch a glimpse of WWII through the French perspective.

2. **Musée Jean-Moulin**: Adjacent to the museum above, Musée Jean-Moulin is also related to WWII. The small museum features exhibits dedicated to the leader of the French Resistance during the Second World War, Jean Moulin, including

memorabilia. Musée Jean-Moulin is open daily, and admission is free of charge.

Les Catacombes

Those with morbid interests never leave Paris without touring the underground ossuaries known worldwide as the creepy Catacombs of Paris. With over six million remains within the catacombs, the labyrinthine place has been given the reputation of The World's Largest Grave. The tunnels and caverns that give Les Catacombes its shape are actually the remains of historical stone mines. If you're not opposed to eeriness, the patterns formed by the skulls and femurs of long-dead French people are a must-see. There's no place in the world quite like Les Catacombes. The entrance to the underground cemetery boasts a black façade that hints at the long, dark descent that is to come. Les Catacombes is not recommended for claustrophobes and young children.

Source:*http://www.feellikehome.cn/en/culture/%E5%B7%B4%E9%BB %8E%E5%9C%B0%E4%B8%8B%E5%A2%93%E7%A9%B4/*

La Coupole

The grandest of Parisian brasseries is often considered to be La Coupole in Montparnasse. Top-of-the-totem-pole artists of the early 1900s regularly dined here, including Jean-Paul Sartre and Pablo Picasso. Characterized by an incredible Art Deco interior and a vast dining room, there is never an empty table at this classic brasserie. If you manage to get a reservation, ask for a table out on the terrace where you can watch the ordinary goings-on of the Montparnasse quarter.

Source: http://www.paris-bistro.com/english/histoire_coupole.html

Marché Edgar Quinet

Shake off the sense of macabre from the Catacombs of Paris with a little light shopping. One of the best ways to experience local living in Montparnasse is to spend a couple of hours at Marché Edgar Quinet. This charming street market has everything you could possibly ask of a market—lunch-to-go, hot crêpes, scarves, and fresh fruit.

Source: http://www.justacote.com/paris-75014/art-et-artisanat/marche-parisien-de-la-creation-1200682.htm

Le Petit Journal Montparnasse

Evenings in Montparnasse are spent by many in music clubs and pubs. A different kind of nightclub experience awaits in Le Petit Journal Montparnasse, owing to the fact that it's a jazz club. It's actually a small chain in Paris, with a second location in the Latin Quarter. Eat a delicious dinner while big bands serenade you with melodic music.

Le Red Light

Finally, a disco club! Despite its name, Red Light isn't a red-light district nightclub. Expect trance, house, and techno mixes here spun by both local and international DJs. During weekends, Le Red Light's multicolored dance floor forms a swaying sea of well-groomed locals revealing their true bonhamie.

Source: http://clubseekr.com/paris-france/redlight/

La Closerie Des Lilas

If you happen to catch a serious case of homesickness--if you're American, that is—this swanky American-style bar is a perfect choice for you. Here, brass plaques detail the exact spot in the bar where early 20th-century luminaries like Picasso and Ernest Hemingway sat. While menu prices are steep in this bar, the rib-eye steak and smoke haddock are worth every euro.

Chapter 8: Classy Saint-Germain-des-Pres

The most classic Parisian neighborhood in the city can be found in the 6th arrondissement at Saint-Germain-des-Pres, an area built around the church of the former abbey. When the town of Saint-Germain was established during the 12th century, it only had 600 inhabitants. Later, it would become the center of Existentialism. Over the centuries, the town grew in population and gradually became the hub of intellectuals, philosophers, artists, actors, and musicians. Today, Saint-Germain-des-Pres is like a city within a city, awash as it is with designer boutiques, urbane streets, opulent art galleries, upscale restaurants, the finest of museums, and multilevel cafés.

Star Attractions

Nearly every landmark in the neighborhood of Saint-Germain-des-Pres is considered a star attraction.

Musée D'orsay

The second most famous museum in France after the Louvre Museum, Musée d'Orsay houses the largest collection of Impressionist masterpieces in the world. Some of the biggest names in the museum include Renoir, Monet, and van Gogh.

The first exhibit haul consisted of 2000 paintings and 600 sculptures. Here, you'll find a total of 86 Monet paintings, 24 van Gogh works, and 81 paintings by Renoir. The top highlights in Musée d'Orsay that you can't leave without seeing include:

1. *The Lion Hunt* by Eugène Delacroix

2. *The Artist's Studio* by Gustave Courbet

3. *The Source* by Jean Auguste Dominique Ingres

4. *The Gleaners* by Jean-François Millet

5. *Olympia* by Édouard Manet

6. *Le déjeuner sur l'herbe* by Claude Monet

7. Self-portrait by Vincent van Gogh

8. *Whistler's Mother* by James McNeill Whistler

9. *L'Absinthe* by Edgar Degas

10. *Dance in the Country* by Pierre-August Renoir

11. *The Church at Auvers* by Vincent van Gogh

12. *The Circus* by Georges Seurat

13. *Female with a Flower* by József Rippl-Rónai

Carrefour De Buci

This busy crossroads in Saint-Germain-des-Pres is home to charming cafés, innumerable shops, and flower markets. During the Reign of Terror, it was here that hundreds upon hundreds of priests and royalists lost their heads to the guillotine. Despite this gruesome event, there isn't a sinister trace in the Carrefour today. With many flowers for sale, freshly baked pastries, and ice cream stands, Carrefour de Buci is the perfect stop after a long morning at Musée d'Orsay.

Institut De France

This highly revered cultural institution is comprised of five *académies*, with the most famous being the Académie française, the guardians of the French language. The Institute also manages no less than 1,000 foundations. While the Institute is a restricted French landmark, many continue to admire the building from the street, particularly its enormous golden dome, which is one of the most impressive landmarks of the Rive Gauche—the southern bank of the River Seine.

Musée Delacroix

Over on Place Furstenberg, you'll come across a small museum that was Eugène Delacroix's final place of residence back in the 1800s. The museum's small collection of artwork includes some of Delacroix's sketches and drawings. An absolute must-see while you're here is the backyard garden where Delacroix built a charming little studio. It was in this studio where he created his amazing frescoes that hang in Église St-Sulpice to this day.

Source: http://cityguide.paris-is-beautiful.com/en/paris/sights/musee-delacroix-the-life-and-work-of-eugene-delacroix/22306

Église Saint-Sulpice

This gigantic 17th century church built in the Baroque architectural style has hosted some interesting nuptials and baptisms in France. Among the most notable are the baptism of Charles Baudelaire and the wedding of Victor Hugo. Since Dan Brown's novel, *The Da Vinci Code*—which was set in France—became a bestseller, thousands upon thousands of tourists flocked to the church's obelisk, which played a key role in the book. The church's asymmetrical towers are a must-see here, along with the 19th-century fountain in the square that Église St-Sulpice occupies. There are more must-sees inside the chapel, particularly two Delacroix frescoes off to the right.

Source:
https://www.flickr.com/photos/mathieufrancoisdubertr and/5558256238

Cour Du Commerce Saint-André

Here is a historic cobbled passageway dotted with cafés, which includes Le Procope, the oldest café in Paris. Cour du Commerce Saint-Andre shows remnants of ancient Paris with its uneven cobblestones and Old World elements in the buildings on the arcade. While you're here, be sure to check out the turret from the 12th century wall of Philippe-Auguste.

Source:http://www.anothertravelguide.com/connoisseu
rs_guide/europe/france/paris/five_legendary_shopping
_passages_in_paris/cour_du_commerce_st-andre/

Jardin Du Luxembourg

A vintage French garden and arboretum, Jardin du Luxembourg houses all that is charming and unique. Promenades lined by uniform trees, landscaped lawns, and colorful flower beds offer a quiet reprieve from the hustle and bustle of surrounding Saint-Germain-des-Pres. Benches line the paths around the expanse of the 56-acre public park where you can sit in deep relaxation while admiring the picturesque 17th century Medici Fountain or the model sailboats on the garden's basin. Jardin du Luxembourg also features swings, pony rides, a merry-go-round, and marionette shows on weekends and Wednesdays.

Palais Du Luxembourg

At the northern part of the Jardin du Luxembourg looms the spectacular Luxembourg Palace whose perfect symmetry adds to its beauty. The palace was built in the early 1600s by French architect Salomon de Brosse, and was meant to be the royal residence of Louis XIII's mother. Today, the palace's current tenants are the French Senate.

Èglise St-Germain-Des-Pres

The neighborhood's namesake is also Paris' oldest church. The Benedictine Abbey of Saint-Germain-des-Pres was founded in the 6th century AD for the sole purpose of—get this—sheltering a small shard of wood which was believed to be a relic of Jesus Christ's cross. In its earliest years, when the area was prone to flooding from the Seine River, the abbey was the burial place of Merovingian kings. The church's Romanesque tower was an 11th century addition that now serves as the quarter's central symbol. Inside, be sure to check out the magnificent 19th-century frescoes in the nave, as well as the Saint Benoit chapel which contains the tomb of French philosopher, René Descartes.

Source: http://en.parisinfo.com/paris-museum-monument/71307/%C3%89glise-Saint-Germain-des-Pr%C3%A9s

The Dance Clubs of St-Germain-Des-Pres

No visit to a Parisian neighborhood would be complete without getting in a little partying. While there are many pubs in the area, we will only focus on the dance clubs, which are said to be the best in Paris.

Chez Castel

Who wouldn't want to dance the night away in a castle? Actually, Chez Castle is a three-story mansion—but it comes close enough! Over the years, this huge labyrinthine bar of free-flowing champagne and vaulted ceilings has seen the crème de la crème of the Parisian cultural scene. When Mick Jagger's in town, Chez Castle is his favorite place to let his hair down at. It's a ritzy bar, so plan ahead. Making reservations at one of the two dining room will make entry a breeze. After a sumptuous dinner, you can retire downstairs in the basement where a huge dance floor awaits.

Le Montana

Just because getting into Le Montana is a huge challenge, it doesn't mean you can't at least *try*. Once you're in, the VIP treatment starts. In fact, Le Montana is a VIP magnet. A-list celebs like Kate Moss and Lenny Kravitz have all partied here. Sipping on enormous cocktails in a nightclub that has a Studio 54 vibe will probably be the cherry on top to your visit to Paris.

Jane Club

If you ask enough locals, you'll discover a stone cellar hidden beneath Saint-Germain-des-Pres. Jane Club actually lies under Alcazar, a popular bar-resto in the neighborhood. The leader of Doors, Jim Morrison, came here frequently to let loose for a night. At Jane Club, expect vintage disco music, funk, and groove. On Sunday afternoons, the club hosts salsa lessons.

Chapter 9: Paris from East to West

Like with everything in the world—light and dark, good and evil—Paris also has two halves that come together to create a harmonic balance: East and West.

Eastern Paris

The neighborhoods that make up Eastern Paris have evolved over the centuries into some of Paris' top destinations. From every cardinal point, Eastern Paris flourishes with funky bars, boutiques, art galleries, and cafés. There are countless things to see here, but here are the top draws of the area:

Bois De Vincennes

Landscaped by Napoléon III, Bois de Vincennes is a large retreat that features expanses of green lawns, a flower garden, an amusement park in spring, and jazz concerts in the summer. An entire well-spent day can be had here due to the many activities and sights hat Bois de Vincennes has to offer, including:

1. **Château de Vincennes**: On the northern fringe of Bois de Vincennes stands a massive medieval castle with roots in the 12th century. Originally a hunting lodge, the French royal fortress is

now a suburb of the metropolis. The castle bore many faces over the centuries—a state prison, a porcelain factory, a nun community. Aside from the high walls of the old château, other imposing features include a dry moat and a 170-foot keep. Tourist activity increased following the restoration of Château de Vincennes to its former glory.

2. **Parc Floral de Paris**:   The floral park in Bois de Vincennes consists of a lake, butterfly garden, and bloom displays sprawled out over 70 acres. Many visitors enjoy the pony rides and paddleboats here.

3. **Parc Zoologique**: Measuring in at 35 acres and containing over 1,000 animals, the Paris Zoological Park is the largest zoo in the city. What makes this zoo so special is the biozone system that provides the zoo animals with a naturalistic habitat according to where they came from. There's a Patagonia for penguins, an African savannah for giraffes, and a free-range aviary for birds. You'll also find a slice of rainforest there, which is housed in a greenhouse that you can actually access.

4. **Palais de la Porte Dorée & Tropical Aquarium**: This Palais in Eastern Paris houses both an immigration museum and an aquarium filled with tropical fish. You'll want to see the ornate façade of the Palais

which is decorated with incredible bas-relief sculptures. More ornate features await you inside: elaborate metal work, well-maintained fixtures, and original marble. Stop by the two salons on the ground floor where one represents Asia, and the other, Africa. The Forum houses mosaics inspired by Africa, so be sure to take a peek.

The upper floors are where you'll find the modern museum that outlines the history of immigration in France. The aquarium, on the other hand, is housed in the basement of the Palais. Expect to see a pair of alligators there from Mississippi. Tickets are only €8 for both attractions—about $9.

Bibliothéque National De France

The National Library of France is a sweeping complex that comprises four L-shaped buildings—meant to represent open books—each built 22 stories high. Intended to be the repository of everything published in France, here is where the most significant printed treasures of the country are stored.

Commissioned by François Mitterrand, former President of France, the library cost a whopping €1,000,000,000 to build. That's nearly 1.2 billion U.S. dollars! The National Library of France contains over 40 million items, including books, newspapers, recordings, patents, stamps, drawings, and manuscripts. One of the must-sees in the library arei the Globes of Coronelli, a pair of 17th-century orbs weighing at two tons each.

Source:
http://www.bnf.fr/en/for/host_an_event_and_filming.
html

Canal Saint-Martin

This underground canal is 4.5 km long, and it was Napoléon I who ordered its construction in 1802. Canal Saint-Martin was dug in the midst of the cholera epidemic as a means of supplying Paris with clean drinking water. For years following its birth, the canal was forgotten by the city. Today, Canal Saint-Martin is a place for Parisians to wander and take picnics on sunny afternoons with their significant others. There's a boat tour you can take that travels from end to end. You'll find a technological marvel a ways down at Rue de Crimée where a drawbridge stands with four huge pulleys. The area near the canal is best explored on foot or on Vélib' bicycles.

Place D'aligre

A quick visit to Place d'Aligre will bring you to two of Paris' best markets: Marché Beauvau and Marché d'Aligre, the latter an outdoor market, and the former a covered one. The dozens of stands here are laden with jams, dried sausages, meats, cheeses, beer, and fresh fruits. Pick up some picnic essentials, then head on over to Square Trousseau.

Musée Édith Piaf

Édith Piaf's petite stature was as famous as her job title as a French cabaret singer. Her tiny two-room apartment where she lived for one year was converted into a museum following her death. Musée Édith Piaf is now a shrine to the talented cabaret singer which displays her personal belongings, such as her handbags, books, dresses, personal letters, and tiny shoes. The walls of the small museum are graced with portraits of the singer done by her artist friends.

Western Paris

Western Paris drastically differs from its eastern counterpart considering the prim and proper quality to the area, as well as newer construction. Here, you'll find that the population consists of a nearly equal mix of locals and foreign expatriates. There's nothing cheap about Western Paris, so keep that in mind when you visit. Despite lying on the costly end of the spectrum, window shopping and admiring the many scenic views here are two very fun and very free activities, thus making a quick visit worth your while.

Bois De Boulogne

The great outdoors is virtually a nonexistent thing wherever big metropolises are concerned. However, Paris is the exception. Bois de Boulogne isn't just your ordinary Parisian park though: it's more like a vast forest landscaped with wooded paths and small lakes. It's *the* place to go when locals are in need of some serious R&R—away

from the buzz of the big city. Expect to cross paths with every type of Parisian here: the chic, the hipster, the ordinary local, cyclists, joggers, picnickers, whole families, rowers—you name it! The highlights of Bois de Boulogne include:

1. **Parc de Bagatelle**: The 18th-century floral garden that is Parc de Bagatelle is home to the prettiest of flowers, a prize-winning rose garden, waterfalls, a Chinese pagoda, and peacocks. Coming here is like being bombarded with a flurry of colors—but in a pleasant way. A stroll through the most beautiful park in Paris will also bring you to Château de Bagatelle, a stunning neoclassical mansion with landscaped gardens going back to 1150. Parc de Bagatelle is the most colorful during the months of April, May, and June.

2. **Le Pré Catelan**: A favorite place to hold wedding receptions and other big celebrations, this ultra-romantic restaurant is home to a special copper beech tree that is one of the largest trees in Paris. There is also a garden in the area known as the Jardin Shakespeare with sprinkles of herbs and flowers which were often mentioned in his famous plays.

3. **Jardin d'Acclimatation**: Located on the northern edge of the Bois de Boulogne, this large garden is Western Paris' version of an amusement park. It's not Disneyland,

but it sure attracts every local preschooler in the city on summer days. There are several rides there, including a few rollercoasters, a small zoo, and a rock-climbing apparatus.

Passy Cemetery

Shaded by chestnut trees, this spooky little Parisian cemetery dates back to 1821. Of the 2600 tombs here, many are occupied by the remains of French like Édouard Manet and aristocrats like Claude Debussy. In fact, Passy Cemetery is considered to be Paris' aristocratic necropolis. Cast your eyes upwards and you'll find the Eiffel Tower looming over you.

Fun Fact: Passy Cemetery is the only cemetery in Paris with a heated waiting room. How thoughtful.

Castel-Béranger

Castel-Beranger made a name for its architect, Hector Guimard, who was a leading representative of the Art Nouveau architectural style. In fact, Castel-Beranger is considered Paris' very first Art Nouveau structure, built as it was with curved lines and inspired by natural forms in flowers and plants. While the house is off-limits to visitors, it's more than rewarding to ogle the front entrance and the fountain in the courtyard.

Source:
https://www.flickr.com/photos/26688567@N04/3538262786

Maison La Roche

Lovers of architecture and design are likely to enjoy Maison la Roche, a villa/museum operated by Fondation le Corbusier. The white structure was built in 1923 as a private villa for a wealthy Swiss banker by French architect, Le Corbusier. Its construction was based on geometric forms and the use of iron and concrete. The showstopper here is the sloping ramp that replaces the traditional staircase. Hour-long private tours can be reserved online.

Musée Marmottan Monet

In the basement of a fancy 19th-century mansion on Rue Louis Boilly, there lives an impressive gallery that flaunts over 300 Monet masterpieces. The collection of Impressionist and post-Impressionist artworks were donated by the great master's son, Michel. Not only does the basement gallery contain the largest collection of Monet pieces, it also houses the famous Wildenstein Collection of illuminated manuscripts. For a manuscript to be considered "illuminated," it has to be decorated with either gold or silver.

Musée Du Vin

A paradise for wine lovers, Musée du Vin features wine artifacts and memorabilia excavated in Paris. The exhibits are displayed in 15th-century vaulted cellars, and includes ancient glassware, old wine bottles, and pottery related to wine-making and storage. Even better, free wine tasting is part of the package. After you've discovered the history of wine, make your way over to the small gift shop selling over 200 different bottles of wine.

Chapter 10: Visiting Glitzy Marais

The historic district of Le Marais is home to many buildings of architectural and historical importance. Several notable hôtels exist here, private mansions of French merchants which are some of Paris' best surviving examples of the Baroque architectural style. Apart from hip galleries, fashion houses, and trendy restaurants, The Marais also plays host to Chinese and Jewish communities. It's also a center of LGBT culture as evidenced by the many cabarets and nightclubs designed for the Parisian LGBT community. A few of the more notable residents of Le Marais in the past were Jim Morrison and Victor Hugo.

Fun Fact: Le Marais started out as a swamp.

The places and monuments of note in Le Marais include:

Archives Nationales

The National Archives is located in a group of buildings comprising Hôtel de Soubise and Hôtel de Rohan in Le Marais. Created in 1790 during the French Revolution, the National Archives of France preserves one of the largest and most important archival collections in the world. Currently, the National Archives houses approximately 252 miles of documents, and growing. The oldest document here is a well-preserved parchment dating back to 695 AD. Several other important highlights in the

National Archives include Louis XVI's diary, the 1598 Edict of Nantes, Napoléon Bonaparte's last will and testament, and the 1648 Treaty of Westphalia.

Source: http://www.sofeminine.co.uk/lifestyle/10-places-to-visit-in-paris-d28657c355378.html

Pletzl

Though slowly fading, Paris' Jewish quarter still retains a fair amount of delis, falafel shops, and traditional Jewish bakeries. The tiny area is only about 1600 ft. × 1600 ft. It became a predominantly Jewish community follow the arrival of hundreds of Jewish immigrants during the late 19th century. During WWII, much of the Jewish population on Parish were sent to death camps. Nowadays, Pletzl is an Orthodox community whose members belong to one of three synagogues in Paris.

Musée Picasso

A must-see for Picasso fans, the museum dedicated to him lies within immense Hôtel Salé. Musée Picasso has a collection of about 100,000 pieces spanning 34 rooms over 41,000 square feet, and includes drawings, documents, and sculptures alongside paintings spanning his entire career. While Picasso's most recognizable works are scattered across Paris in different museums, Musée Picasso contains his most treasured paintings and sculptures.

Place Des Vosges

Of all the plazas in Paris, Place des Vosges is the oldest—and to many Parisians, the finest. Henri IV built the square in the early 1600s, embodying the first European program of urban planning. Nowadays, there are nine brick-and-stone houses on either side of Place des Vosges. Victor Hugo once lived at No.6, so be sure to check out that house. At the base of these houses is a traditional Parisian arcade lined with boutiques, cafés, and art galleries. There's also a synagogue here, as well as several fancy hotels. Chestnut trees line a formal garden in the square. On the vast expanse of emerald green grass, you'll find Parisians and tourists sprawled out, picnicking, or enjoying a good book.

Source: http://www.paris-architecture.info/PA-034.htm

Maison De Victor Hugo

If you've read *Les Misérables* or *The Hunchback of Notre Dame*, you've heard of Victor Hugo, the multitalented and most celebrated author in France. His old private mansion on Place des Vosges where he lived for 16 years is now a museum dedicated to the French author. If the exhibits inside don't catch your interest, the ornate furnishings and the blood-red walls certainly will.

You'll pass through an Asian-style living room decked out in Chinese wooden panels, followed by a dark, medieval dining room. Upstairs is where all the magic is, including manuscripts and early editions of *Les Misérables* and *The Hunchback of Notre Dame*. The bedroom where Hugo died is sumptuously decorated. There, you'll find his short bed and the tall desk where he wrote much of *Les Misérables*.

Musée Carnavalet

There is no better place to discover the evolution of Paris than the Carnavalet Museum. Everything you ever wanted to know about the history of Paris is here. Established in 1880, the museum occupies two adjacent mansions, Hôtel Carnavalet and Hôtel Le Peletier de Saint-Fargeau, and houses nearly 600,000 exhibits. There are 2,600 paintings, 300,000 engravings, 20,000 drawings and sketches, 150,000 photographs, 800 pieces of furniture, and 2,000 sculptures. Of those, here are the show-stopping exhibits of Musée Carnavalet that you *have* to see—no excuses:

- In the courtyard, a sculpture of Louis XVI—as if you can even miss its magnificence.

- The very canoes that the very first colony in Paris, the Parisii, used called pirogues, which were made from a single tree trunk.

- A bottle from the 4th century used for wine, honey, or perfume.

- Scale model of the Île de la Cité.

- An elaborate 13th-century chest thought to hail from a royal abbey.

- 14th-century sculpture of Virgin Mary's head depicting a contemplative appearance.

- 16th-century paintings depicting the Renaissance era and the Wars of Religion.

- 17th-century painting of Pont Neuf, a bridge, that shows Parisians on horseback.

- Paintings of Madame de Sévigné, the most beautiful woman in Paris.

- Jacques-Louis David's uncompleted paintings during the French Revolution.

- Paintings of Mirabeau, Danton, and Robespierre—famous actors during the Revolution.

- A painting by Pierre-Antoine Demauchy representing the fate of death by guillotine.

- Marie-Antoinette's personal effects.

- Napoléon Bonaparte's toiletries.

- Paintings representing 19th-century Paris.

- *The Seizing of the Louvre* by Jean-Louis Bézard.

- Louis Napoléon Bonaparte's ornate cradle.

- Belle Epoque posters.

- Émile Zola's gold watch-chronometer.

- Photographs of 20th-century Paris.

Musée Cognacq-Jay

Hôtel Donon, a 16th-century Rococo-style mansion, houses one of the loveliest museums in Paris, Musée Cognacq-Jay. The free tour through the lavish museum provides visitors a rare glimpse into the lifestyle of the wealthy Parisians of the 19th century. Musée Cognacq-Jay's collection of fine art and decorative pieces contains about 1,200 items spread out over four floors. The main exhibits on the second floor are tiny medallion portraits; on the third floor, inlaid snuff boxes, perfume bottles, and ornate pocket watches. You'll also come across jewels, ceramics, cigar cutters, and sewing boxes.

Source: http://en.parisinfo.com/paris-museum-monument/71087/Mus%C3%A9e-Cognacq-Jay

Musée De La Chasse Et De La Nature

Within a 17th-century structure called Hôtel de Guénégaud is Paris' most bizarre museums. The Museum of Hunting and Nature is as fascinating as it's odd, and critics say it's one of the most inventive museums in Paris. The exhibits here celebrate the relationship between humans and nature through the practice of hunting. Multiple well-stocked rooms focus on a specific themes. Exhibits include taxidermied animals, ancient weaponry, hunting accessories, and representations of nature scenes and hunting. Look out for the curio cabinet dedicated to unicorns, the albino boar head mounted on the wall, and the ceiling in one of the rooms that's made up of owl feathers.

Source: http://en.parisinfo.com/paris-museum-monument/71275/Mus%C3%A9e-de-la-Chasse-et-de-la-Nature

Hôtel De Sully

Over on Rue Saint-Antoine, there stands a magnificent Baroque mansion built in the Louis XIII style. Hôtel de Sully was classified as a historical monument in the late 1800s. In the 1950s, new owners—namely, the Center des

Monuments Nationaux—restored the private mansion into the gem it is today. While it's off-limits to visitors, Hôtel de Sully is eye-candy enough to warrant a visit and a quick stroll through its public garden, which is just as lovely.

Hôtel De Sens

Beautiful. Stunning. Hopelessly romantic. This blue-roofed castle dates back to 1475 AD and is one of three medieval private residences remaining in Paris. Once the home of Queen Margot, first wife of Henry IV, Hôtel de Sens has had its share of infamy, owing to the Queen who was known for her many lovers. While you're here, look for the lodged cannonball in the front façade which commemorates a battle that took place here in 1830. Also, don't leave without taking a gander over at the elegant garden in the rear.

Home Of Nicolas Flamel

Nicolas Flamel was the French scribe whose Philosopher's Stone is the source of immortality in the Harry Potter series. Built in 1407, his private residence has a mystical history. It was here that Nicolas Flamel dabbled in alchemy and the mystical arts. Legend has it that he discovered the sorceror's stone, which enabled him to achieve immortality. Today, Flamel's home serves as a complex containing apartments and a restaurant.

Le Marais Nightlife

As it turns out, the quarter isn't just home to tons of museums: Le Marais also has a huge party scene. By nightfall, throngs of Parisians pour out onto the streets of Le Marais to enjoy a night out at one of the many pubs and nightclubs in the area. The best clubs to hit include:

La Belle Hortense

An evening at La Belle Hortense will most likely consist of a drink in a bookstore setting. It's a welcome reprieve from the noisy bars that make up the nightlife at Le Marais. Bookworms will enjoy the literary atmosphere here as the interior of the bar is lined with shelves upon shelves of books both new and old, with a several rare editions included. An enormous menu of quality wine is available here.

Grazie

Anyone who's had the opportunity to dine at Grazie calls the restaurant the best pizza joint in Paris. A mellow vibe awaits inside, along with great drinks and a friendly staff. Grazie is the perfect weeknight hangout for a group of friends.

Little Red Door

So named due to the little red door that marks the

joint's entrance, this restaurant is dark, cozy, sophisticated, and stylish. Old oversized leather armchairs make for comfortable seating—without looking the least bit pretentious. The bartenders are super friendly and the atmosphere will make you feel like VIP. Highly recommended for tourists who don't mind shelling out €15 for a drink.

As previously mentioned, Le Marais has a big LGBT culture whose members are some of the most friendly and outgoing Parisians in the entire city. If you don't mind partying in an LGBT atmosphere, there are plenty of gay and lesbian bars at Le Marais. Tourist favorites include: a lesbian bar called So What! that happily welcomes newcomers; 3W Kafé, meaning "women with women"; Café Cox, a prime gay pickup joint; and La Perle, a bustling nightclub where heterosexuals and people of the LGBT community come to mingle without no judgement whatsoever.

Chapter 11: A Peaceful Respite at the Islands

The only two islands in Paris, Île de la Cité and Île Saint-Louis, can be found at the heart of Paris in the River Seine. It's recommended to either visit these two small islands first and foremost, or save them for the last day of your trip. Both islands are so picturesque that they could easily pass off as postcards.

Île de la Cité

Considered the center of Paris, Île de la Cité is the location where the medieval city was re-founded. The western end of the island is home to a palace with the opposite end dominated by the Notre Dame. Between the two stands a number of buildings, and the northern edge of the island remains residential.

Notre Dame Cathedral

This iconic French Gothic powerhouse anchors Île de la Cité and is a symbol of Paris. It's not the oldest church in France, nor the biggest—but it certainly is the most well-known church in the region, and rivals all others in architectural scope and beauty. Construction began in 1163, today's Notre Dame embodies architectural harmony. Two enormous columns from the 12th century stand like guards at the entrance of cathedral, acting as supporters of the towers. Down the nave, you'll spot the 12th-century statue of Our Lady of Paris. The Treasury lies south of the choir, containing reliquaries, garments, and crucifixes. Be sure to check out the Crypte Archéologique, an archaeological museum.

Fun Fact: The Emmanuel bell in the south tower of Notre Dame Cathedral weighs 13 tons.

Source:
http://www.aviewoncities.com/paris/notredame.htm

Place Dauphine

Place Dauphine is a V-shaped public square--one of Paris' oldest. Laid out in the early 1600s, the square is now a peaceful respite from the hustle and bustle of the metropolis. Place Dauphine is ideal for a romantic dinner on one of the restaurant terraces there during the spring and summer seasons.

s

Source:
https://www.flickr.com/photos/meteorry/304
6294176

Sainte-Chapelle

This beautiful, still-active medieval chapel is considered one of the highest achievements of French Gothic architecture. King Louis IX commissioned the erection of the chapel in the 1200s in order to house his Passion Relics collection—including Jesus Christ's Crown of Thorns. The stained glass windows here are must-sees as they are the qualities that give Saint-Chapelle its jewelry box appearance.

Palais De Justice

Once the seat of French royalty and now a place of justice, Palais de Justice is one of the most important official buildings in Paris. Its façade is impressive and the courtyard here is amazing. Be sure to take plenty of pictures in front of the golden gates of the building.

Conciergerie
This former prison once served as the place where blueblood victims of the French Revolution like Marie-Antoinette were held while awaiting death by guillotine. In 1914, the Conciergerie became a national historical monument. Nowadays, it's a tourist hotspot, with long queues outside of Marie-Antoinette's recreated cell. Cast your gaze to the stained glass windows in the chapel where you might be able to see the doomed queen's initials. There's a courtyard outside where you'll come across the fountain in which female prisoners washed their clothes. Guided tours are available for free, however, they are only in French.

Source:
http://www.aviewoncities.com/paris/conciergerie.htm

Hôtel-Dicu

Hôtel-Dieu is a large general hospital regarded as the oldest in Paris. Not only that: Hôtel-Dieu is the oldest hospital worldwide that's still running today. The facility is comprised of two buildings, one built in the 7th century, and the other, ten centuries later. These days, the hospital operates on a public care system. Hôtel-Dieu isn't exactly a tourist destination, but being able to say you've visited the oldest hospital in the city is certainly worth it.

Ancien Cloître Quartier

Hidden within the shadows of the Notre Dame Cathedral is this little neighborhood from the Middle Ages, which still retains its medieval charm. One of the more notable residents of Ancien Cloître Quartier was Ludwig Bemelmans, the creator of the beloved *Madeleine* books.

ÎLE SAINT-LOUIS

Pont Saint-Louis takes you to the Île Saint-Louis, which is considered the best places in Paris to wander around. Unlike Île de la Cité, there isn't much to see here besides a handful of narrow streets, small hotels, eateries, small art galleries, and several specialty shops.

Fun Fact: Back in the 1930s, the residents of Île Saint-Louis declared the island an independent republic.

Source: http://davidphenry.com/Paris/paris557.htm

Conclusion

Thank you again for downloading this book!
I hope this travel guide was useful, and that it provided you with sufficient enough information to make your visit to Paris rewarding and worthwhile.

Paris is the ultimate destination where tourists of every culture can find solace and an unforgettable experience. Whether you're a fashion buff, a lover of architecture, a history major, a wild soul, a simple soul, or an adventure seeker, there are tons of sights in Paris that conforms to your tastes. The City of Light is one of those magical places where mystery and beauty lurk in every corner, and old harmonizes with new to create a dream world whose remnants stay with you forever.

The next step is to take this book with you and enjoy as much of Paris as you can.

Good luck and *bon voyage*!

Additional bonus material below featuring some content from other travel guides in this series. Enjoy!

New Zealand Travel Guide

Introduction

The 29 regions of New Zealand extend in over 1,600 kilometers throughout the country's two main islands, the North Island (Te Ika-a-Māui) and the South Island (Te Waipounamu). Every destination in New Zealand offers a distinctive character, and because the country is compact, you can reach every destination easily during your visit.

Some of the most popular regions of New Zealand that are worth your time, energy, and money include Auckland, Bay of Islands, Christchurch, Franz Josef, Nelson, Queenstown, Rotorua, Taupo, Waitomo, and Wellington.

Auckland

Auckland is the largest city in New Zealand. It is also the country's main transport hub. During your travel, make sure to visit Auckland as it offers a superb experience in dining, shopping, and natural wonders. Auckland has an immense harbor, vibrant cityscape, and serene islands, which make it extremely astonishing. You can never run out of water, wildlife, and urban activities when you visit Auckland.

Top Things You Should Not Miss in Auckland

Auckland is the largest city in New Zealand. It is also the country's main transport hub. During your travel, make sure to visit Auckland as it offers a superb experience in dining, shopping, and natural wonders. Auckland has an immense harbor, vibrant cityscape, and serene islands, which make it extremely astonishing. You can never run out of water, wildlife, and urban activities when you visit Auckland.

Explore the Hauraki Gulf. Make sure to visit and explore this amazing gulf that offers a wide range of sea life as well as exciting water activities. You can go fishing, sailing, whale-watching, scuba diving, and boating.

Bungee Jumping. AJ Hackett, the inventor of Bungee jumps, operates one of the first Bungee jumps in the world. In this Auckland Bungee jump, you will jump off a bridge going into the harbor. You can also try the 143-meter Nevis jump in Queenstown for a higher and more exhilarating jump.

Sky Tower Experience. The Sky Tower is more than 1,000 feet high. In fact, it is the tallest tower in the southern hemisphere. Here, you will have amazing panoramic views of Auckland. The Sky Tower also has a revolving restaurant at its top and an access to the city's casino.

Stop by the Auckland Domain.   After a long day of activities, you can stop by the Auckland Domain, a huge, lovely park in Auckland.   It is usually filled with people who play sports, run, or simply take a break during summer months.   The Auckland Domain has sub-gardens and nice walks.

Shopping at the Otara Flea Market.   **If** you are in Auckland on a Saturday, pass by this Maori and Polynesian market where you can find unique food, clothes, and other local items with some amazing deals.

Unwind at the Waitakere Ranges.   If you are into water, make sure to head to the Waitakere Ranges where you can find rugged yet beautiful beaches and impressive waterfalls. You can join a popular day trip, which is normally for locals, especially when you are in Auckland during the summer time.

Take Your Family to the Auckland Zoo. If you are traveling with your kids, you can take them to this zoo, which has 500 animals, several different habitats including the Rainforest and Pridelands, and 150 animal species.   The Auckland region offers a wide range of wildlife that you should not miss.

Explore the MOTAT.   The Museum of Transport and Technology or MOTAT is an interactive museum, which is home to over

300,000 technology as well as transportation-related objects. It is just a few minutes away from the Auckland Zoo. Its admission fee is $15 NZD.

Head to the North Shore. Every local in Auckland will suggest this place, especially during the night. It has an extremely active and vibrant nightlife. It is the region's main beach area and is popular among surfers.

Travel Back in Time at the Howick Historical Village. This "living museum" is the perfect place if you want to go back in time. It houses items from the mid-1800s. The staff of this museum is dressed in costumes and speaks in different accents.

Underwater Experience at the Kelly Tarlton's Sea Life Aquarium. Look through the depths at a wide range of stingrays, sharks, and fish that swim around you as you go through a long see-through tunnel. This place also lets you experience the Antarctic through its permanent winter exhibit.

Head to the Gannet Colony at Muriwai. This place allows you to view thousands of breeding gannet birds that nest between the black sand dunes of the Muriwai beach. The perfect time to visit this place is between March and August. It has two viewing decks for bird watching. If you are not so much into birds, you can go biking, hiking, or surfing in Muriwai. There is also a surf school if you want to learn how to surf on the spot.

Brave the Waikumete Cemetery. This is the largest cemetery in New Zealand and home to several heritage buildings such as the Corban family mausoleum. Many visitors and travelers find it interesting to walk through the cemetery as the dates on most of its tombstones are quite unbelievable. There are available guided tours every first Sunday of the month.

Christchurch

Christchurch is known as the "garden city." It is home to most of the country's beautifully-sculpted gardens and parks similar to the Victorian England. This region is multi-cultural and has a vibrant student population. It is also one of New Zealand's popular destinations for backpackers.

In spite of its severe damage during the earthquake in 2011, which caused a number of attractions to close, Christchurch is being rebuilt slowly.

Top Things You Should Not Miss in Christchurch

Head to the Antarctic Center.   This place, which is near the airport is perfect if you have an interest in Antarctica.   It offers pertinent information of the continent's wildlife and the environment.   It also has a simulated Antarctic environment.   Here, you are given the chance to ride in a Hägglund Antarctic vehicle.

Christchurch Gondola Ride.   Located in the southern suburbs of Christchurch, this gondola ride lets you see various views of the city as well as the surrounding areas.

Willowbank Wildlife Reserve. This place is popular for its amazing nocturnal kiwi tours.   It is a wildlife park that is home to a number of native birds.

Cathedral Square. This place is the town's main center in which you will find markets and fairs.   Most locals hang out in this place.   An event transpires every weekend.   Currently, the cathedral is still closed as it was ruined during the earthquake.

Port Hills. The trails in this place is one way to catch excellent views of the region as well as the Banks Peninsula and the Southern Alps.   You have the choice to walk or bike in the trails. Most locals also pick this spot for doing outdoor exercises.

Explore the Canterbury Museum. This is a museum with free admission. You can take your kids to this place, which features Maori, colonial and natural history, visiting exhibitions, and Antarctic exploration display.

Spend Time at the Hagley Park's Leafy Glades. This place is filled with colorful themed flower beds in its Botanic Gardens. It also has beautiful English trees that you can admire as you walk, run, cycle, or relax in the place. You can also experience the tranquility that the Avon River provides. At night, the place is likely to be filled with runners and joggers.

Go Shopping at the Lyttelton Farmers Market. This place offers an authentic market where you can find the freshest, seasonal produce. Most locals contribute their own fresh produce while others shop. Here, you can find organic food such as cheeses, eggs, bread, honey, and relishes among others.

Explore the Bone Dude. In this place, you will be fascinated with bone carving. You also get the chance to do your own bone carving. You can join a session that runs once a day from 12 to 4 in the afternoon during Mondays through Fridays and 10 to 1 pm on Saturdays. The owner has built a temporary studio in his home garage after his original studio way destroyed during the earthquake.

Visit the Mona Vale. This place is an Elizabethan-style home with an immense manicured land. Inside the house, pre-made picnics are available. You need to order them a day before due to attention to detail they work on into every meal. In addition, most locals order from them, especially during weekends and holidays.

Walk through SoMo. This area is located at the south of Moorhouse Avenue. It is considered as the most creative area in the region. It consists of the neighborhoods of Addington and Sydenham. Here, you can spend time exploring the streets, checking out live music during the evenings, or eating at unique restaurants and cafes including Burgers & Beers and Honey Pot Cafe.

Get Familiar with the Maori Culture. You can have the chance to know more about the traditional Maori Culture by exploring Kotane. It is a cultural center found on the Willowbank Wildlife Reserve. The admission fee to this place is around 165 NZD; however, it already includes a performance show with upscale production, a four-course dinner, and a tour of the wildlife reserve and the village.

Franz Josef. In 1865, Franz Josef, which is popular for its glacier located about 3 miles from town, was first explored. The town became the jumping off point for all the glaciers. Franz

Josef's glacier is one of the South Island's major highlights. You can get a chance to walk across its glaciers as well as explore ice tunnels.

Top Things You Should Not Miss in Franz Josef

Try the Heli-Hiking. This place allows you to hike on the ice and have a scenic flight over the glacier. If you want to reach the remote parts of the glacier, you can join tour groups.

Explore the Hukawai Glacier Center. This place features an audiovisual display about the glaciers of New Zealand. It also offers a glacier experience, geology and mythology of the Maori, and information on the wildlife. The center also has an indoor ice-climbing wall.

Go Rafting on the Perth and Whataroa Rivers. Both rivers are located on the north of Franz Josef. It is best to visit them during summer. The rivers are the perfect spot for one-day whitewater rafting. They are amidst forests and wilderness. These rivers have Class IV and V rapids.

Go Trekking on the Glacier. One of the best things to do in Franz Josef is to trek on the glacier for one full day. You will be amazed by the views as well as the remote ice tunnels around the area.

Try Soaking in the Glacier Hot Pools. If you want a dose of rejuvenation, visit the series of outdoor thermal baths. Head to these glacier hot pools after an intense hiking or trekking activity. Soak in the hot pools or get a massage to loosen up your body.

Go Horseback Trail Riding. If you are tired of walking, you can do a horseback trail ride and enjoy some extra mileage to your tour. There are trips available in Franz Josef, which run for six hours. Some tours are also available, which allow you to horseback along farm lands and remote beaches.

Go Skydiving. If you want a truly exhilarating activity, jump out of a plane at 18,000 feet to have a single view of the mountains, glaciers, rain forest, and rivers. Franz Josef is one of the few places across the globe that offers this elevation. Prices for skydiving start around 300 NZD.

Go Kayaking. You can rent kayaks on Lake Mapourika for 60 NZD or join a kayaking tour for three hours for 115 NZD. The tour offers an interesting trip across the lake, kiwi sanctuaries, rainforest, and glacial walls.

Go Fishing. You can go fishing on the mountain lakes that offer opportunities for anglers. You can also fish for trout in the region's slow-moving creeks.

Explore the Historic Swinging Bridge.
You can stop and walk the historic swinging bridge if you are driving toward the glacier. The bridge offers a magnificent view of the valley and provides a thrilling experience as you walk across the wobbling structure. It is also your chance to stretch your legs for a few minutes as you continue driving towards the glacier.

Rotorua

Rotorua is considered as the main destination for Maori cultural experiences, nature walks, luxury spas, and tours to smelly geysers. It is located in North Island and popular among locals and tourists. Although there is not much you can do in town except for a few restaurants, bars, and shops, you will find all the exciting activities when you travel from Rotorua.

Top Things You Should Not Miss in Rotorua

Discover the Maori Culture. While you are in the area, you can join various educational tours and watch a wide range of cultural shows that feature the Maori culture. All tours feature the Tamaki Maori Village, which you should not miss. In addition, most of the tours offered already include food packages. Tours include either small or big groups and vary in length.

Have a Great Time at the Lake. The city is set next to a lake where an island sits in the middle. It is a good idea to spend some time to relax, especially in the afternoon. You can cruise along the lake or hike in the island.

Explore the Whaka Thermal Reserve. This place is ideal if you are fond of geysers. It is split into two parts and provides information about the areas natural history and geology. The guided tours include the entrance fee for the reserve. The tourist part of the reserve is the Te Puia, which is close to town.

Take a Dip in Hot Baths. There are a number of sulfurous springs in Rotorua, which means that there are also plenty of hot springs where you can relax. One of these is the huge Polynesia Spa, which features an all-day access and free drinks. There is also the Blue Baths, which features a heated pool.

Try Zorbing. One of the most popular activities among locals and tourists in Rotorua is zorbing. You will be put into a giant transparent ball and rolled down the hill. It works like a washing machine where the clothes go round and round inside. There is also an option where you can add water inside your ball.

Wellington

Wellington is New Zealand's capital city and the third most populous urban area of the country. The city's architecture as well as unique vibe makes it a place of character and personality. It features great food, activities, nightlife, and an amazing harbor.

Top Things You Should Not Miss in Wellington

Visit the Beehive & Parliament House. The Beehive, which is a government building and the adjacent Parliament House are near the train station. A free, guided tour is available so you can see parts of the buildings that are open to the public.

Stop by the National Archives. This place houses most of the significant documents of New Zealand. It has the 1893 Women's Suffrage Petition and the original Treaty of Waitangi. This is the perfect place if you are interested in the country's history.

Visit the Old St. Paul's Cathedral. This cathedral was built from native timbers. It features colonial Gothic architecture.

Tour the Karori Wildlife Sanctuary. This place is a conservation project that houses a number of endangered and rare wildlife of New

Zealand including kaka and weka birds, kiwi, and saddleback. It has more than 22 miles of trails with great views. You can also explore its 19th century goldmine.

Visit the Te Papa. This is one of New Zealand's huge national museums. It features Maori and Colonial history as well as a broad section on New Zealand's geology. Entrance to the museum is free of charge.

Explore the Wellington Zoo. If you are traveling with kids, you can head to the oldest zoo in New Zealand, which houses a wide variety of Asian, African, and native wildlife. The entrance fee is about 32 NZD.

Drop by the Lookout Points. The city of Wellington is surrounded by hills; thus, it has plenty of good views. You can head to various lookout points in the city through riding a bus, bike, or cable car.

Discover New Zealand's Maritime History at the Museum of Wellington City. This museum is great for people who are into maritime history. It also features the history of Wellington. Admission is free.

Explore the Carter Observatory. This full-dome planetarium is located near the Botanic Gardens. Check out this place during the day to see different cosmos shows or during the night for some stargazing.   The planetarium also features exhibits and a gift shop.

Stop by the Botanic Gardens.   This place is great to go out for an afternoon walk or a picnic. You can reach the top by taking the Cable Car located in Lambton Quay.   You can also walk to reach the top of the gardens.   This place is full of colorful flowers, great views, and lawns where you can relax, especially on a clear day.

Explore the Wildlife at Zealandia.   This place is located at the west of Wellington.   It is a wildlife sanctuary that houses some of New Zealand's native birds including hihi, kiwi, and saddleback among others.   There is also an exhibition center that you can visit after you are done touring outside.

See a Movie at the New Zealand Film Archive. This place is a library that was established in 1981.   It houses more than 30,000 movies that can be seen for free on the library's big screen.   There is also a small cafe as well as a gallery that you can check out.

Please purchase this book from the Kindle store to find out more about New Zealand.

Sydney Travel Guide

The Most Beautiful Parts of Sydney

Sydney's rich history dates back to a thousand years ago. During that time, the entire Australian archipelago was still inhabited by different aboriginal tribes. Most of these tribes still inhabit the same regions throughout the country. But most importantly, they have managed to hold on to their ancient way of life. The first Caucasian settlers set foot in Sydney in the late 1800s. These settlers consisted of English convicts, their armed guard, and high-ranking officials of the British crown.

The convicts were immediately put to work in building the foundations of a town that now serves as Australia's biggest and most bustling city. Some of the buildings that the convicts established are still standing to this day and can mostly be found in a part of the city known as The Rocks. Throughout the years, the city has effectively shed its past as a penal colony. Its government has managed to place Sydney at the top of the map for the world's most well-developed cities. But some remnants of the past are still apparent if you know where to look.

There are many historical buildings that are sprinkled around the city. There are also certain areas in and outside the city center that are revered for its ancient history, specifically the history of its indigenous people. Aside from its history, the beauty of Sydney is also manifested by the parts of it that are closest to nature. The endless sky serves as an amazingly blue backdrop to the endless stretches of white sandy beaches and sparkling blue seawater.

The following list has been assembled in order to make it easier for tourists to decide which parts of Sydney to go to first. Every item on the list is a place that people just have to visit at least once in their lifetimes.

Sydney Opera House

Did you know that 90% of tourists almost automatically go to the Sydney Opera House as soon as they set foot in the city. It is Australia's biggest architectural icon and the most recognizable Australian building in the world. No one would believe that you've been to Sydney if you don't have a photo taken at the Opera House. However, the building's beauty belies the tumultuous process that its engineers and architects had to undergo.

The difficulties of building such an amazing work of art are manifested on the fact that it took 16 years for the Sydney Opera House to be completed. It even came to a point where its architect Jorn Utzon had a falling out with the government. This led to Utzon's absence during the unveiling of his most memorable masterpiece in 1973. A reconciliation didn't come about until the early 1990's, which means that Utzon only got to see the finished product decades after he first started working on it.

It now stands at the forefront of Australia's ranking in the world of art and technological innovation. However, the outside of the Sydney Opera House is not the only thing that deserves notice. It also serves as a venue where various performing arts groups get to showcase their talents.

The Opera House's value to the world of art and modern creativity is also evidenced by the fact that the roof sails often serve as a backdrop where lights are projected into by creative lighting artists who want to showcase their talents. This light projection show on the Opera House's domes is mostly done during special Australian holidays as well as during a festival known as the Vivid Sydney.

Sydney Harbour Bridge

The Sydney Harbour Bridge is one of Australia's most well-known and photographed landmarks and is a must see when visiting Sydney. When touring the harbour or catching one of the popular Sydney ferries one gets a stunning view of the Bridge and the Opera house.

The Sydney Harbor Bridge is the world's largest (but not the longest) steel arch bridge with the top of the bridge standing 134 metres above the harbour and connects the Sydney CBD with North Shore business and residential areas.

To locals of Sydney, it is fondly known by the locals as the 'Coathanger' because of its arches which are an integral part of its iconic design.

Just to fill you in on a little of the history involving the construction of this iconic bridge. Construction of the Sydney Harbour Bridge began in 1924 and took 1,400 men eight years to build at a cost of $4.2 million, and in its construction six million hand driven rivets and 53,000 tonnes of steel were used. The bridge has a total length of 1,149 metres and a height of 141 metres and was finally opened on March 19th 1932 by Premier Jack Lang. A small interesting fact is that the bridge has huge hinges to absorb the expansion caused by the hot Sydney sun. You will see them on either side of the bridge at the footings of the Pylons.

Sydney Harbour Bridge Pylon Lookout

When at the bridge you must visit the Pylon Lookout so that you can take in some fantastic views of the city of Sydney, and the beautiful harbour and its surrounds.

There are 200 stairs to the Pylon Lookout which is 87 metres above sea level, but on the way up there are 3 levels of exhibits where you will discover the history and construction of the Sydney Harbour Bridge, the men who built it, and the vision of JJC Bradfield, chief engineer.

Pylon admission prices are at the time of writing this travel guide are as follows:

General Admission (13 years and over)	$13.00
Concession (Seniors & Student)	$8.50
Children (5 to 12 years, inclusive)	$6.50
Children (4 years and under)	FREE

Opening hours are 7 days a week, from 10.00am to 5.00pm, with the only day that the lookout is closed is Christmas Day.

Sydney Harbour Bridge – BridgeClimb

The Sydney Harbour BridgeClimb is fantastic, if you are not scared of heights and in definitely one of the 'must dos' while on a trip to Sydney and visiting the Sydney Harbour Bridge. I have climbed experienced the BridgeClimb and survived, as have many royal and celebrity visitors. Certainly a must do, if you have a 'bucket list'.

So what does this experience involve? This involves climbing the Sydney Harbour Bridge with an expert guide so that you can me amazed by the views Get amazing views from the summit of the bridge – 14 metres up. Scared now? Not to worry, you have several options for your climb, including a sampler tour that goes halfway up which takes approximately 1.5 hours to the full summit tour and climb which will take approximately 3.5 hrs. No matter which option you choose, ascending this famous landmark gives you a spectacular perspective on Sydney and an exhilarating sense of achievement.

As a climber you will be provided with protective clothing appropriate to the prevailing weather conditions, and are given an orientation briefing before climbing. If you wish to participate in this climb, please ensure that you have not been drinking any alcohol as you will need to have a test for a blood alcohol reading before the climb. Safety is paramount! During the climb, you are secured to the bridge by a wire lifeline. Each climb begins on the eastern side of the bridge and ascends to the top. At the summit, the group crosses to the western side of the arch for the descent.

Bridge Climb Pricing starts a$148 during the work week for adults and $118 per child.

Bondi Beach

Whether the goal is admiring the antics of surfers as they battle the waves or admiring a colorful sunset, Bondi beach is always a top choice. Tourists can also take leisurely walks along the famous Bondi to Coogee coastline. They can start at Bondi Icebergs and go on a leisurely stroll that would take approximately 2 hours and end at Coogee beach.

There are loads of beautiful views to take in between these two beaches. If you're lucky, you might also get to see some whales whose migration pattern starts in May and ends in November. There are also several other beaches in between Bondi and Coogee beach to stop and admire. These include Mackenzie's Point Beach, Bronte Beach and Clovelly Beach.

Each beach has its own attractions, which includes quaint cafés and beautiful sandstone formations. The Bondi-Coogee walkway is perfect for families who want to take a few hours of bonding time together, groups of friends looking for some adventure, couples who just want to take a romantic stroll, and amateur photographers who are on the lookout for the perfect shot.

Sydney Botanic Gardens

The garden stands on 30 hectares of land and is located right in the heart of Sydney's Central Business District (CBD). It is a welcome oasis for tourists who are tired of the fast-paced lifestyle of the urban jungle. There are hundreds of different plant species on the garden, as well as various species of animals that are mostly native to Australia. These animals include flying foxes, possums, and various bird species such as Black Cockatoo and the Buff-banded Rail.

After checking out the Botanic Garden, walk a few steps over to the Government House. The house has been standing since the late 1800's and is currently in use as the governor's residence. While at the House, be sure to check out the historic eastern terrace. Hundreds of balls and events have been held on that terrace, most of which were attended by the world's foremost VIPs. The terrace also provides an unrivaled view of Sydney Harbour, which makes it a perfect spot for selfies.

Blue Mountains

This is one of the many UNESCO World Heritage Sites in Australia. It is located just a short drive away from the metropolitan area. The Blue Mountains is a welcome retreat for every tourist who is tired of life in the big city. The mountain gets its name from the way that the entire range appears to be bluish when viewed from afar. This bluish tinge is due to the fact that the entire range is covered by eucalyptus trees.

These trees disperse oil onto the atmosphere, which then combine with water vapor and dust particles. These combined elements then scatter bluish rays of light over the range, which to the human eye could simply be construed as the color of the mountains itself. The Blue Mountains is inhabited by 6 aborigine groups:

- Darkinjung
- Darug
- Gundungurra
- Wanaruah
- Wiradjuri
- Tharawal Nations

These aborigines have inhabited separate sections of the Blue Mountains long before the first European settlers came. They are also acknowledged as the traditional owners of the Blue Mountains.

Aside from its cultural significance, the mountain range also has a uniquely diverse ecosystem with habitats that include wetlands, grasslands, and localized swamps. If you want to get close to a Koala or want to know what a long-nosed Potoroo looks like, then head out to the Blue Mountains ASAP.

There are many other selfie-perfect spots around Sydney that every tourist would surely fall in love with. Take a leisurely stroll around the CBD to discover cafés with quirky themes and other uniquely-themed restaurants tucked into the hustle and bustle of the city. Or you can also travel to the outer edges of the city to see some of the glorious sights. These sights will be discussed further in another chapter along with all the outdoor activities that you can do there.

Please purchase this book from the Kindle store to find out more about Sydney.

London Travel Guide

London: Nothing Short of Amazing

The jolly old City of London is still one of the biggest tourist sites in the world today. When we say London or City of London, we're referring to the entire metropolis not just the original square that the Romans built. It's not the largest city in the world, well, not anymore. The other cities around it have grown in size and proportion but London still remains just as enchanting today as in the days when it was still the largest metropolis in the entire world.

If you think you know English well enough, then you ought to have a go at pronouncing the names of the different places here. You may be surprised to learn a new thing or two about the language. Other than the mere majesty of the place and the royalty of the names of different places, the British capital presents an amazing journey especially to those who will be visiting here for the first time.

A Wonderful Mix of Pretty Much Everything

Diversity is the biggest thing you'll find in London. It has a multicultural mix with people coming from pretty much anywhere in the world. It's a melting pot of different people with different points of view. It is as noisy as it is vibrant and that makes the place even more wonderful to visit. Why visit London? One of the biggest reasons is that the city opens windows where you can catch a glimpse of the world. But that's not the only reason why people visit the city – there's more to it, which is why it is one of the most popular tourist centers in the world. Here are some of the reasons why people come here in droves:

- History Encapsulated: Have you ever wondered what an actual Roman city looks like? London was founded during Roman times and they called the place Londinium – well, that basically just refers to the original 1.12 square mile core of the city. Its medieval boundaries still stand today. The city's history spans about two millennia. Within its boundaries are historical sites and landmarks that offer visitors various glimpses of history long lost.

- Theater Scene: The city itself attracts the best talent from different countries. London's theater scene is considered the best in the entire world. In fact, the best acting talents have been drawn here to perform live on stage. There are classic plays, musicals, and other new works put on the spot light. Don't be surprised to see some of the best actors in the movies to take the stage.

- The Pub Circuit: If you're a night owl then you will love the pub scene here in London. Some bars are just bars where you can get a drink and mingle with the local population. Others are pubs where you can get some hot steamy action. You'll definitely enjoy the rooftop bars and the many riverside pubs where you can enjoy the scenic views as you enjoy a lovely night cap.

- Gastronomic Adventure: It is no secret that London is one of the best culinary circuits anywhere on earth. You can sample the finest culinary masterpieces from different cuisines right here within the city limits. You can start your day with a tasteful breakfast from a traditional British restaurant, have lunch in a Michelin-starred restaurant to delight your taste buds, and finally party the night away in one of the many gastropubs and enjoy the company of the locals.

- Shopping: If you love signature brands and if you love to get your hands on the latest fashion trends then you're in luck – you just found the Mecca of the fashion industry when you come over to the wild streets of London. You can find pretty much everything from chic boutiques to iconic signature stores in Westfield Stratford. However, there are other side options that are just as good. They're easy to find; just turn at the next corner and you'll find well-known names such as Harrods and the other flagship stores along Oxford Street.

- Free Attractions: Whenever you visit a leading tourist destination in the world, you should get ready to burn some cash – a lot of things can be a bit expensive the way they charge tourists nowadays. However, the good news about London is that there are some pockets of resistance, as it were, and there are areas where things are still free. London has some of the best free attractions that any tourist will love. You can spend time in culturally rich museums, enjoy lovely afternoons at a park, or just get a panoramic view of the Thames without spending a dime – more of that in the chapters that follow.

- Sports: One of the reasons why people flock to London is to watch the action at the different sports events. The country's capital has some of the best sports venues in the world. If you like to see some of the best hard hitters in the hard court then you can witness the action at the Wimbledon. If you like a slightly quieter playing field then you can visit Lord's Cricket Ground. If you're a big fan of football then you must see a game when one is scheduled at Wembley Stadium.

A Few Travel Tips

This pretty much gives you a bird's eye view of what to see and experience in London. The city has so much to offer and it can be a bit bewildering sometimes. If there is one tip that we can give you at this point it would be to peruse the different attractions mentioned in this book and then pick your favorites. After that, you can schedule your itinerary. That way you have a short list of places you want to see for yourself when you get there. However, make sure to have a plan B, you know, just in case a restaurant or a museum will be closed for maintenance by the time you get there. At least you have an alternative when the unexpected happens.

London: The Best the City Can Offer

In this chapter we'll give you a bird's eye view of the best attractions you'll find in the city. London offers a plethora of sites and experiences – you may run out of time on your holiday just to visit them all. The idea is not to try and see everything in one trip. You can actually just visit some of the best attractions. If everything proved to be such a thrill, which it is by the way, then you can visit the rest of the sites on your next vacation or holiday from work.

In this chapter you'll get to see what many consider as the best attractions in London. What you'll find below are brief summaries of the different attractions. Some of the more important details about each attraction will be provided. The focus here is to give you an idea of the adventures that await you.

Madame Tussauds

So, you want to rub elbows with royalty, eh? You might just get your wish at Madame Tussauds. Well, you're not going to meet them in person but you're getting the next best thing – their lifelike wax figures.

Madame Tussauds offer its visitors with interactive displays and life-like wax figures of royalty and celebrities alike. They have a total of

14 interactive displays and you get to meet and greet with more than 300 celebrities from all over the world.

From an audience with Her Majesty the Queen to a trip aboard the Millennium Falcon, you'll fulfill your childhood fancies here and more. You can even strike a pose with your favorite icons including your sports heroes.

Adult tickets cost £31 per person while children's tickets cost £25 per child. They open their doors to the general public from 9:30 in the morning to 5:30 in the afternoon. However, during the peak times (holidays and weekends) they only operate from 9 am to 4 pm. Please check their official website for other important dates, schedules, and announcements.

Madame Tussauds is at Marylebone Road, London, NW1 5LR. Contact numbers are 0871 894 3000. You can take the Baker Street train and get off at Marylebone to get to the place.

Royal Museums Greenwich

The Royal Museums Greenwich is a consortium of different museums that now operate under this present name. All four businesses and points of interest were located in the same heritage site anyway. The aforementioned museums include Cutty Sark, the Royal Observatory, the Queen's House, and the National Maritime Museum.

It's one of the best places to visit here in London simply because it's free. Of course, there's more to it than that; the National Maritime Museum is actually the biggest maritime museum in the world. There was a time when it was considered that the country that controls the seas controls the world. Well, that was when maritime travel was the only international mode of transport available to man.

The English Empire at one point was a leading contender, the Spanish with their armada, was another. Any rate, England has a huge maritime history. If you're a fan of sailing and the life at sea (don't forget the pirates!) then this place will be a huge treat – especially for the kids.

You can actually spend several hours with your entire family just to see everything that these four institutions have to offer. Remember that the sites and attractions at the Royal Museums Greenwich do not only entertain – they amaze.
Admission is usually free. However, there are temporary and seasonal attractions that require an entry fee. These sites usually open at 10 am and close at 5 pm. The National Maritime Museum is along Romney Road with phone numbers +44 (0)20 8312 6565. The Cutty Sark is along King William Walk with telephone numbers +44 (0)20 8312 6608. The Queen's House is also along Romney Road with phone numbers +44 (0)20 8312 6565. The Royal Observatory is located within Greenwich Park

with phone numbers +44 (0)20 8312 6565.

Harrods

If you're after designer clothing and you have the cash to burn then Harrods is the most recommended place to get signature clothing. It was established back in 1834. It's one of the most impressive upmarket department stores anywhere. The building itself occupies 5 acres providing more than 330 stores/departments. That simply makes it the largest department store in Europe.

Harrods is located at 87-135 Brompton Rd. You can contact them through phone at +44 20 7730 1234.

Tower of London

No trip to London will be complete without a visit to the Tower of London. This tower has a rich 900 year history – great for history buffs and anyone interested in the lives of kings and queens plus the knights who fell in love with them. You'll get to see the itty gritty details of an actual royal palace. The tour comes complete with a tour of the private zoo, the king's jewel house, the arsenal chambers, and of course the place of execution. You will even be treated to a view of the king's bed chamber. If you're lucky you can even catch a glimpse of the Crown Jewels on your visit.

Admission is free for all children who are below 5 years of age. Adult admission is £22 while tickets for children are priced at £10. The place is usually open all year round from around 9 am to 5 am.

Opening and closing times may change at different times of the year so check out any announcements at their official website. The Tower of London's address is Tower Hill, London, EC3N 4AB; telephone numbers are 0844 482 7777.

Big Ben

London's Big Ben is one of the iconic landmarks in the city. It's actually the clock tower at the Houses of Parliament. No visit to London will be complete without a visit here. Here's a little bit of trivia: the name Big Ben was originally given to the bell inside the clock tower and not the entire clock tower itself. Well, eventually everyone referred to the entire tower as "Big Ben" and the name caught on.

This massive clock has rarely stopped even after a bomb hit the Commons during World War II. The official name of the tower was actually changed to Elizabeth Tower in June of 2012. The name change was instituted to honor the diamond jubilee of Her Majesty Queen Elizabeth II.

You can't walk up to the tower itself but you can always visit the Houses of Parliament, which basically houses the clock tower.

Victoria and Albert Museum

Are you a fan of the arts? You'll love the V&A if you are. They have art works and artifacts gathered from all around the world. The art exhibits do not only showcase the usual sculpture and paintings. You'll find art in other mediums such as textile, metalwork, as well as furniture. Note that most of the exhibits you'll find here are free. However, there are times when they may showcase some special areas that will require visitors to purchase tickets.

Entry to the Victoria and Albert Museum is free. However, do take note that they have special exhibits on occasion, which will require an entry fee. The place is open daily from 10 am to 5:45 pm. They also have extended operating hours during Fridays wherein they remain open until 10 in the evening. Note that the place is closed during holidays. The V&A Museum is located at Cromwell Road, South Kensington, London, SW7 2RL. Their phone numbers are +44 (0)20 7942 2000.

The Science Museum

This is one of the places here in London that will be a great treat for the kids. Well, the adults will enjoy the exhibits and attractions here as well. Well, they won't call it the Science Museum without featuring the scientific discoveries and contributions from the greatest British minds. A lot of the exhibits here are interactive. You even get to end your tour with a feature film at the Imax cinema.

Expect the Science Museum to be a bit crowded when you visit there. It's the most popular museum of technology and science in Europe. Here you'll find the actual Apollo 10 space capsule among the more than 15,000 of technological exhibits on display.

They also have a lot of interactive displays where you and your kids will learn the deepest questions that science tries to answer. Another fun part of the tour here is the simulators (both in 3D and 4D). You'll get to feel what it's like to be on an actual spacecraft launching from earth.

Entry into the Science Museum is free. However, you will have to pay a small fee to get onboard a simulator or if you want to watch the film in the IMAX 3D Cinema. The official address of this museum is Exhibition Road, London, SW7 2DD. Their telephone numbers are 0870 8704 868. They're open daily from 10 in the morning to 6 pm.

The London Eye

If you're a Marvel Comic movie fan then you will recognize this huge "Ferris Wheel" like object (I would hesitate to call it just a contraption – it's a marvel in itself) from the Fantastic 4 movie. The Coca-Cola London Eye is one of the really curious things in London's skyline. It's also one of the best places to go in case you're interested in taking panoramic views of the entire metropolis. Unfortunately, a ride on the London Eye isn't exactly free. You'll have to pay some £20 or so just to hop on a ride. But that is money well spent – the breathtaking views are well worth it.

Admission for adults at the Coca Cola London eye is £20.70 for adults and £14 for children. Note that all children that are below 4 feet are given free admission. If you have a party of 15 people then all of you get a 10% discount in the entry fee. The place is open daily from 10 am to 9 pm. The place is closed during the holidays.

The London Eye is located at Riverside Building, County Hall, Westminster Bridge Road, London, SE1 7PB. Telephone numbers are 0871 781 3000.

Natural History Museum

Now, this is another interesting place for the kids. Note that there are a lot of attractions in London that are great for families. They have quite an extensive collection in their dinosaur exhibit. Have you ever wondered how big a blue whale would look like if one was sitting right in front of you? Well, you'll find that out here in the Natural History Museum because they have one on display for you to see.

Other than the displays, you can also speak with actual scientists from Darwin Centre Cocoon that usually offers free lectures, forums, and other exhibits. You can even watch these scientists live as they perform actual experiments. Anything you need to ask about nature and science, they'll be happy to oblige.

Admission in the Natural History Museum is free. However, they also host special events – those require an entry fee. The museum is open daily from 10 am to 5:50 pm. They're also closed during the holidays.

The museum's address is Cromwell Road, London, SW7 5BD. The phone numbers are +44 (0)20 7942 500.

National Gallery

The National Gallery in London is another big treat for art lovers. If you love the classics from 13th to 19th century then the pieces on display here will make your heart skip a beat. You'll find works by artists like da Vinci, Renoir, Van Gogh, and many more. Admissions are generally free but they also have exhibitions that will require visitors to get tickets.

Admission in the National Gallery is actually free. However, they do have special exhibitions on occasion and those require entry fees. Adult fees for special exhibits are priced at £13.20. Student passes are at £6. The gallery is open daily from 10 am to 4 pm. During Fridays, the place will remain open until 9 pm. The place is located at Trafalgar

Square, London, WC2N 5DN. Telephone numbers are +44 (0)20 7747 2885.

Buckingham Palace

No trip to the land of kings will be complete without visiting the royalty's abode, right? Buckingham Palace is the place to beat in case you want to see royal regalia at its best. Just the décor is enough to leave your jaw hanging. Unfortunately, the doors of the palace are only open to the general public at certain times of the year. Note: summer openings are greatly anticipated. Now, even if you miss the opportunity to see the palace's interior, you can still witness the ceremonial Changing the Guard.

A visit to Buckingham Palace requires a small entry fee. The ticket price for adults is pegged at £20.50 and £11.80 for children. They also offer family tickets, which cost £52.80 per group. They also offer special tickets like the Royal Day Out ticket which gives visitors special access to certain rooms and sections in the palace that aren't usually open to the public.

Buckingham Palace is usually open daily from 9:30 am to 6:30 pm. They also have extended openings during certain times of the year. Summer is the best time to visit the palace grounds since they often have special offers during the summer months. Its official address is London, Buckingham Palace, SW1A 1AA.

Official phone numbers are +44 (0)20 7766 7300.

Warner Bros. Studio Tour London

Do you want to see what Harry Potter's version of London looks like? Then head off to the Warner Bros. Studios. Enjoy the walking tour and see some of the coveted behind the scenes attractions. You can explore the world in which Harry and his friends had their adventures and more. Exhibits include a tour of Dumbledore's office, the Nimbus 2000 (sorry, you can't hop on that for a ride), and you finally get to step into and discover the wonders of the Great Hall. Visitors will also see how actual animatronics technology work. See how life size figures of different Hogwarts creatures are made to look real and alive in front of the camera.

Entry fees to the Warner Bros. Studio Tour London are £63 for adults and £58 for children. Note that there are no tickets sold at the entrance – that means you have to purchase them in advance via the internet. Note also that visits are scheduled; that means you have to arrive on time for your scheduled tour.

Warner Bros. Studio Tour London is located at Studio Tour Drive, Leavesden, WD25 7LR. Their telephone numbers are 0845 084 0900.

Tower Bridge

Tower Bridge was built between 1886 and 1894. It spans the River Thames, connecting the London boroughs of Tower Hamlets (north side) and Southwark (south side). The bridge combines elements of a suspension bridge design with elements of a bascule bridge design. It has two towers linked by two walkways and suspended sections to either side of the towers, stretching towards the banks of the Thames.

Tower Bridge was originally designed by Sir Horace Jones, the City Architect at the time and more than 400 workers were required to build the bridge which is 244 metres long and each tower is 65 metres high with the pedestrian walkways are over 40 metres above the river when it's at high tide.

The main bridge deck carries two lanes of road traffic between two low-level pedestrian walkways across both suspension spans and the opening bascule section of the bridge, with the walkways separated from the roadway by fences. The roadway passes through each of the two towers, whilst the low-level walkways pass around the outside of the towers.

Many people think that Tower Bridge is called London Bridge, when in fact they are two different crossings

Bonus Content

As a token of our appreciation Grand Reveur Publications would like to give you access to our exclusive bonus content (including free eBooks!).

Exclusive pre-release access to our latest eBooks Free Grand Reveur eBooks during promotional periods.

A method ANYONE can use to publish their own book and make passive income

To receive this bonus content visit the following web site:

https://ignorelimits.leadpages.net/grandreveur publications/

As this is a limited time offer it would be a shame to miss out, I recommend grabbing these bonuses before reading on.

CPSIA information can be obtained at www.ICGtesting.com
Printed in the USA
LVOW10s1818170316

479616LV00029B/771/P